The Art and Craft of
Coffee

To Larry McManus, 1941–2009, whose encouragement and creativity
started my involvement in the world of coffee.

First published in the United States of America by
Quarry Books, a member of
Quayside Publishing Group
100 Cummings Center
Suite 406-L
Beverly, Massachusetts 01915-6101
Telephone: (978) 282-9590
Fax: (978) 283-2742
www.quarrybooks.com

Library of Congress Cataloging-in-Publication Data

Sinnott, Kevin.
  The art and craft of coffee : an enthusiast's guide to selecting, roasting, and brewing exquisite coffee / Kevin Sinnott.
      p. cm.
  ISBN-13: 978-1-59253-563-7
  ISBN-10: 1-59253-563-1
  1. Coffee 2. Coffee brewing. I. Title.
  TX415.S526 2010
  641.3'373—dc22

                                                                                                    2009052418

ISBN-13: 978-1-59253-563-7
ISBN-10: 1-59253-563-1

10 9 8 7 6 5 4 3

Cover Design: Rockport Publishers
Cover Image: Petroff Photography
Design and Layout: Visible Logic, Inc.
Photography: Petroff Photography, except pages 12, 15, 16, 18, 24, 27, 29, 31, and 37 by Geoff Watts of Intelligentsia Coffee
The recipes on page 168 are copyright Jura, www.jura.com.

Printed in China

The Art and Craft of

Coffee

An Enthusiast's Guide to Selecting, Roasting, and Brewing Exquisite Coffee

Kevin Sinnott

BEVERLY MASSACHUSETTS

QUARRY BOOKS

CONTENTS

INTRODUCTION

It is possible to taste the volcanic lava from Sumatra and to smell the spice fields of India. I know of no better way to travel the world than through a passion for coffee.

Do you remember your first cup of coffee? Mine was on the first date I had with a young woman who is now my wife. We saw Romeo and Juliet one crisp, autumn evening, and her oversize college sweater and the aroma from the chain coffee shop are sensual memoires I can still conjure today.

My next most vivid coffee memory came after my first son was born. We had no money, and we drank House of Millar Mocha Java from the grocery store. I also ground it at the grocery store because I didn't own a grinder. I brewed it in a basic brewer we'd gotten as a wedding present. I remember it tasting rich and elegant.

One day, I noticed the House of Millar wasn't on the neighborhood store's shelves anymore. I was devastated. I drove to a nearby store, and I bought all of the bags left on their shelves. I stored all but one in the freezer.

Meanwhile, a dedicated coffee bean store opened nearby. The store's owner, Guy, seemed like a laid-back artsy sort, who liked nothing more than to spend his days sampling the various coffees. I became a frequent customer.

Trouble was, as much as I liked Guy's coffee at his shop, I could never get it to taste the same at home. My wife even started questioning whether we should spend the extra money on Guy's beans. While I stood my ground (grounds?) on buying good beans, I privately realized the coffee was better when Guy brewed it in his commercial equipment.

I knew it was time to upgrade my home equipment. I bought a burr grinder on clearance and discovered a Chemex at a thrift shop. Each time I improved my brewing equipment, the coffee tasted better. I have never looked back, and I have spent decades mastering the brewing process to ensure the best possible cup of coffee is brewed every time.

This book taps into my decades of coffee brewing experience and teaches you how to make café-quality coffee at home in direct, easy-to-follow instructions—without dogma.

Coffee and wine are more alike than coffee and tea. As with grapes, every nuance possible can be affected by the earth and climate from which coffee comes. These differences can last all the way to the final flavor and aroma from your cup.

A few key themes are explored in these pages:

• Grinding is critical to the brewing process. The job of any coffee grinder is to divide the beans into same-size pieces. This might seem simple, but grinders are the Achilles' heel of many a home-brewing station. Here, you will learn how best to achieve proper grounds at home.

• Brewing coffee is half art and half chemistry—or alchemy. The exact portions of ground coffee to water, the water temperature and the water's contact time with the grounds all affect the flavor of the final coffee. It is possible to make two very different tasting beverages from the same beans using different brewing methods or using two identical brewers and simply altering the variables with each brewer.

• Espresso shares many qualities with brewed coffee, but there are some differences that affect the selection of beans, roasting, grinding, and (certainly) brewing that grants it its own chapter.

• We treat coffee botany lightly becuase the topic could fill a book in itself. Just note that most coffee in the world comes from three or four original plants, and there are a number of variations designed mostly to allow coffee to flourish in a range of climates. While consumers have little control over these variations, I predict they will become more important as they discover the flavor effects each species has on the final cup. Some higher-quality coffee roasters are starting to list the coffee species (such as bourbon, typica, and caturra) on their packaging.

If there's one thought I hope you come away with after reading this book, it is that coffee should be consumed for pleasure. I used to joke that I'd prefer the worst cup of coffee with my wife to the best cup with her mother. (I no longer say this because my mother-in-law and I have become very close.)

Remember, coffee gives you the chance to travel the world, exploring culture, history, and terroir through a culinary lens. After you read this book, your coffee will taste better than ever and possibly better than you even thought it could.

PART ONE THE BEANS

1 KNOWING YOUR COFFEE BEANS

COFFEE is like wine—hundreds of varieties line the shelves, their names offering little to help you differentiate dark from light or good from bad. And much like wine, the flavor of coffee depends on its source: the bean. Understanding this aspect of coffee is the first step to understanding the whole process. The bean contains the genetic flavor profile of each flavor note. But how do you select the best beans? From what varieties can you choose?

Many variables define each coffee bean type. This chapter focuses on the differences between unroasted beans. In other words, the names and phrases you likely know—French roast, hazelnut, fine ground—show up in later chapters. To find and enjoy the best coffee, you need to start with the basics.

By the end of this chapter, you will know the following:

- What to ask when shopping for coffee, whether at a specialty coffee retail store, at your local grocer, or online

- The difference between coffee varieties. Some differences mean distinctive flavor profiles; others indicate different coffee qualities.

- An understanding of many of the world's coffee-growing regions

< Raw coffee ships in jute or burlap bags. Recently, innovative foil packaging has proven to protect coffee from outside aromas and moisture that affect beans. Further testing and cost will ultimately determine whether burlap will be replaced, but for now burlap rules.

The History of Coffee

To move forward with coffee knowledge, it's important to look back at coffee's history. Little is recorded about its origins, though many (like us) venture educated guesses.

Coffee's Discovery

There's the often-circulated, unproven story of Kaldi, a goat herder who observed one of his herd chewing on coffee cherries. Soon, the goat began to dance.

Kaldi, following his animal's good judgment, chewed some cherries and found himself similarly energized. Kaldi takes the coffee cherries to a local monastery, where the monks toss them into a fire. Instead of destroying this tool of the Devil, the fire accidentally roasts them, creating the first coffee.

What has been proven is the plant's likely regional birthplace, either in Ethiopia or Yemen. The word sounds similar to Ethiopia's Kaffa region, prompting

wide acceptance that the term coffee derived from there. Starting in around 600 CE, men of certain nomadic tribes drank a crushed coffee cherry/ ghee (butter) mixture to energize before battles. Muslim monks (before Islam released an "official" statement) used the crushed cherries before all-night prayer vigils to reap similar energizing benefits.

Religion Meets Coffee

Acceptance of coffee wasn't always so widespread. Religious groups had to understand and allow this new, strange drink. Islam wrestled with it first: Should the drink be treated like alcohol, a forbidden, euphoric, but intoxicating drink to avoid, or recognized as a gentle, nutritious, refreshing alternative to alcohol? The latter won out and coffee prevailed throughout the Islamic world.

Its first use as a heated beverage likely occurred around the tenth century in Turkey, where other beverages made by brewing toasted herbs and teas first became popular. With its close proximity and active trade with Europeans, Turkey helped coffee spread into the Christian/European world.

The Catholic Church, which seldom delves officially into dietary matters, became embroiled in whether Christians should partake of this new drink. When pressed for an answer, the reigning pope, Clement VIII, insisted on a sip. He instantly proclaimed coffee a good tasting and healthful beverage for Christians. Jewish law, which frequently declares various foods kosher (in accordance with the religion's rules and customs), deemed coffee allowable.

Coffee Goes Public

The 1500s brought with them the world's first coffeehouses in present-day Saudi Arabia. With the go-ahead from the church, peasants could now enjoy coffee without fear of persecution. These public places, known as the Kaveh Kanes, offered Muslim men a sanctuary in which to congregate. Similarly, Europe's coffeehouses were the province of male bonding, fostering business and political activities. With coffee's increased popularity came increased clout. In the 1500s, the Turkish placed such importance on coffee that a woman could divorce her husband for failure to provide it for her; it was considered as vital as food and shelter.

Coffee Growing No Longer Just for Arabia

By the late 1600s, coffee—all of which came from Yemen and Ethiopia—was Europeans' drink of choice. But with the explosion of maritime shipping and colonialism at its peak, nations wanted to control their own coffee-drinking destiny by sourcing beans from home. This control meant independence and new industry.

The Dutch, in the mid-1600s, tried first. When they won control of Ceylon (present-day Sri Lanka) in 1658, they began a full-scale coffee industry there; they finally had land on which coffee would grow. In 1699, Dutch colonialists began production in Indonesia, bringing coffee-plant cuttings from India to Java. Curiously, the Dutch did not guard their coffee plant cuttings as carefully as they could have, storing a number in the Amsterdam Botanical Garden and purportedly giving some to other European countries as gifts.

< Meet tomorrow's coffee trees: coffee seedlings.

If the Dutch shocked historians with their generosity, even more stunning was the liberality of France's King Louis XIV. Louis distributed cuttings from his single cutting (a gift from the Dutch government in 1714) to various French colonies in the New World. King Louis entrusted infantry officer Captain Gabriel Mathieu de Clieu to take the cuttings to French colonies. This was no easy task. A challenging sea journey became near impossible when coupled with trying to keep a plant alive onboard. De Clieu detailed in his log battles with pirates, a spy on board, storms, drought, and heat. But all along, he nurtured the shoot. Indeed, he claimed his plant survived the difficult voyage only because he shared his water rations with it.

When the boat reached Martinique, the chosen spot for France's first planting, de Clieu had to make the single plant survive and prosper. He succeeded, motivating local farmers to make coffee, not cocoa, their primary crop. King Louis, who had previously felt lukewarm about de Clieu, honored the man with governorship of Martinique. Meanwhile, cuttings from de Clieu's plant spread. Soon, all neighboring Caribbean islands possessed coffee, and a new industry was born.

Brazil's capture of the precious coffee plant from which to build its own empire is equally dramatic. In one account, a Brazilian lieutenant seduces the wife of the governor of French Guiana to obtain a coffee plant cutting supposedly concealed within a bouquet of flowers. This scheme, in 1827, spawned the entire Brazilian coffee industry.

Coffee Meets the Industrial Revolution

The Industrial Revolution, which sought to centralize every process, prompted a shift in coffee making from small batch roasters to the use of large roasters and a packaging system that allowed advance roasting and grinding—known as the coffee can. Coffee pioneer John Arbuckle created the first canned coffee in 1865.

The new consumer age focused on maximizing convenience. By the 1920s, most urban consumers in America and Europe were buying roasted and ground cans of coffee. Technology was improving, making coffee far easier to churn out. Commercial coffee roasters produced more coffee in larger batches and less time. Suddenly, a few could meet the masses' coffee needs.

The loser in this new era was the coffee's freshness. Instant coffee, popularized by Nestle in the 1930s, brought the ultimate flavor loss. Like so many foods before it, coffee became a commodity, stressing convenience over taste.

FRENCH COFFEE, ENGLISH TEA

France has long had a flourishing coffee culture, but England is known more for its tea. This may seem strange, especially considering England's early coffeehouse development. The story is complex. Both France and England developed colonial coffee agriculture. France planted in the Caribbean and on Africa's Ivory Coast; England planted in Ceylon, (modern-day Sri Lanka).

Ceylon was, at one time, plush with coffee fields. But leaf rust, a fungus that destroys coffee, hit hard. Instead of planting new coffee crops, Ceylon planted tea—which was immune to the leaf rust virus. Back home in England, it became patriotic and fashionable to drink tea. And though France had lower quality coffee than England, the country had plentiful, quality milk. Gradually, France became known for coffee and England (and most of its colonies) for tea.

Fresh-picked coffee cherries, looking delicious enough to eat.

In the 1950s and 60s, coffee joined the ranks of TV dinners, canned fruits and vegetables, and other processed foods. Producing countries started mixing the best coffee with all other coffee. Some great coffee stayed separate from the masses, but that was an exception. The refrigerator's presence in homes harmed coffee just as much, making available soda and juices—competing instant gratification products.

The Seventies and Beyond

In the 1970s, the focus shifted from convenience back to taste. Baby boomers, born between 1944 and 1961, embraced specialty foods as part of the return to natural, self-absorbed diets and increased leisure time. The new focus touched on every aspect of home cuisine, including coffee. Coupled with this

consumer trend was the invention of the air-assisted small batch coffee roasters. Now, even shopping malls could house fresh roasted coffee beans.

Plus, the coffee-shop-alternative-lifestyle-image fit Baby Boomers, who had grown up with beatniks reading poetry in urban coffeehouses. Coffeehouse culture emerged in American cities such as Seattle and Boston. Berkeley, California–based Peet's Coffee and Tea, founded by Dutch immigrant Alfred Peet, is most often credited for the specialty coffee revolution.

But the rise of specialty coffee meant more than a return of social coffeehouses. Small batch roasters began investigating how to find the best beans. During the nineteenth and much of the twentieth century, coffee-growing countries encouraged selling beans from country to country rather than from

farm to roaster. New relationships formed. Specialty green coffee buyers began purchasing micro-lots and requesting particular farms' beans. Small farms started earning awards and honors for their beans.

Specialty coffee appliances underwent a revolution as well. Automatic drip brewing machines replaced the electric percolator, which was once a mainstay in most American households and accused by many connoisseurs of destroying the subtler coffee tastes.

Commodity versus Specialty Coffee

Today's commercial coffee production may seem like one big mass of beans, but generally, it splits worldwide into commodity and specialty coffee.

Commodity coffee includes everything from price-conscious diner coffee to coffee produced to add its caffeine extract to aspirin. This coffee's taste is secondary to its purpose, which is to deliver a brown beverage containing caffeine. It may seem unromantic perhaps, but understanding this aspect is necessary to understanding coffee and its terminology.

Specialty coffee is grown, processed, shipped, roasted, sold, and brewed with taste as the primary focus. In general, specialty coffee prices vary so much because they consider production cost as well as taste, a subjective variable. Overall commodity market conditions affect specialty coffee's price.

No actual botanical or legal distinctions exist between commodity and specialty coffees. In this book, we focus primarily on specialty coffees—not to be snobby, but because it's more practical.

Separating beans from cherries the old-fashioned way. This process can be done using larger machines, but this one does the job just as well, and it is conveniently portable. Note the ripe cherries in the foreground awaiting their turn.

Coffee Plants and Botanical Classifications

Let's break down the coffee plant. Botanically, coffee is a shrub, part of the Rubiaceae family. Only three of the seventy-three classified species—Arabica, Robusta, and Liberica—have commercial significance in today's world market. They yield from three to twelve tons (2.8 to 10.9 metric tons) per hectare (2.5 acres). Each cultivar requires a specific number of trees to create descendants.

Arabica

Arabica (*Coffea arabica*), the original plant discovered and cultivated for today's coffee beverage, likely originated in present-day Ethiopia. Though Arabica naturally contains the least caffeine, it possesses the subtlest, most desirable flavors.

Arabica trees typically grow between twelve and twenty feet (3.7 and 6 m) high. Most Arabica coffee picking happens by hand. This is partly due to its growth on mountainous land usually unreachable by machine but mostly because a human coffee picker, using a ladder or a hook, chooses the ripest beans. The best farms pick multiple times a season—three is common—to ensure selection of ripe beans.

There are two varieties of Arabica: Bourbon and Typica. From these two varieties other subvarieties, known as cultivars, are derived.

Bourbon

Many people consider coffee produced by this Arabica heirloom the world's best quality. The problem is that Bourbon requires significant space and care, is disease-prone, and its trees, which take longer to bear fruit, have a short life cycle. Bourbon yields roughly one-third more beans than Typica and its cherries ripen faster, but they are more fragile. Bourbon grows best at elevations between 3,500 and 6,500 feet (1,067 to 1,981 m).

Typica

This variety, often considered the original coffee type, has a cone shape and grows at a slant. Though it grows well (slightly better than Bourbon) and taller than most varietals, ten to thirteen feet (3 to 4 m) tall, it tends toward lower yields. For the scope of this book, consider Bourbon and Typica equals.

Caturra

This cultivar, discovered in Brazil and developed from Bourbon cuttings, was designed as a hardy, yet high-maintenance plant. It flourishes at elevations below 3,500 feet (1,067 m) with easy-to-pick cherries that grow close to the ground. Many well-regarded coffee growing countries, such as Costa Rica, plant almost entirely Caturra.

Other Arabica Varietals

Which cultivar a coffee farm plants depends on the farm's terroir, climate, and disease resistance first, with productivity and yield considered second. Quality follows last, if at all, because a coffee that won't grow isn't a good crop.

A list of the main Arabica cultivars (in addition to Bourbon, Typica, and Caturra) and their basic characteristics follows:

Blue Mountain
The unique Blue Mountain cultivar, the majority of which grows in Jamaica, likely descends from Typica, though its exact origins remain unknown. It is a long bean, known for its huge flavor and disease-resistance, but it does not flourish in other geographic regions. Blue Mountain does best at altitudes above 5,000 feet (1,524 m).

Catimor

Catimor, developed in Portugal in the 1950s, comes from the Timor cultivar. It grows quickly, produces high yields at middle altitudes, and is particularly resistant to rust disease, making it attractive to many farmers. It is a hybrid of Arabia and Robusta, and it is considered incapable of being the best coffee. It needs significant fertilization and rainfall.

Catuai

This variety is a cross between Caturra and the hearty Mundo novo. It is wind-resistant and sturdy, making it suitable for stormy environments. Like Caturra, it is high-maintenance but produces quality coffee.

Maragogype

This Typica descendant, first found in Brazil, grows bigger and taller than heirloom cultivars. It doesn't produce a high yield, but its beans are large. Two descendants of Mariogype are more popular. Pacamara is a hyrbrid with Paca, grown in Panama. It offers large size and prize-winning aroma and taste. Geisha is a hybrid of Maragogype from Ethiopia, first grown in the early twentieth century. It is prized by connoisseurs seeking a large bean and voluptuous flavor.

Pache Comum

This Guatemala-discovered cultivar likely descends from Typica, though its coffee is not considered as high quality. This hardy plant does well at elevations between 3,500 and 6,000 feet (1,067 and 1,827 m).

Timor

Named for an Indonesian island and known for its parentage of the Catimor cultivar, Timor was believed discovered during the 1860s coffee blight. It is a cross between Arabica and Robusta. Some industry mavens consider Timor a savior, as it seems to offer the best Arabica taste with Robusta's disease resistance. But it is dreaded by some as offering too little taste and is, by them, considered Robusta disguised as Arabica.

Had a serious plant disease not spread throughout several key coffee growing regions in the 1860s, Arabica might have remained the world's only cultivated coffee. Instead two other coffee genera developed: Robusta and Liberica.

Robusta

Coffee growers once touted Robusta (*Coffea canephora*), with twice Arabica's caffeine content and a high disease resistance, as Arabica's best replacement. Robusta coffee trees are shorter, making their fruit easier to pick, and they require less space between trees, allowing more to fit on one plot. In terms of care and feeding, Robusta quickly became a world commodity.

On the flip side, Robusta offers none of Arabica's flavor nuance. There are good Robustas, but they are comparable in quality to low-grade Arabica. This coffee type is sold and traded as a commodity in the United States and Europe. The best is sold almost exclusively as espresso blends. Robusta's best attribute is its body.

Liberica

In the 1870s, as leaf rust diseases ran amok through Arabica coffee fields, author Francis Thurber predicted that Liberica (*Coffea liberica*) could replace Arabica. His prediction never came true. Liberica's flavor didn't match the best Arabica coffee, and its per-plant yield disappointed next to Robusta's. Meanwhile, hardier Arabica variants such as Caturra replaced more vulnerable Bourbon growths.

Today, Liberica thrives in Southeast Asia. Occasionally, a small green amount is available online, but it has no real market penetration in the United States or Europe.

< Ripe coffee cherries. This photo shows the color that coffee connoisseurs imagine all their beans are at harvest time.

Coffee Varieties by Grade (or Marketing Scare Tactics)

Phrases such as *grade*, *fair trade*, and *organic* grace many a coffee bean label. Any savvy buyer should know the terms' real meanings. For information about processing coffee beans, see chapter 2, "Selecting Coffee Beans."

Grade

In the commercial world, grade is important. But at the specialty level few connoisseurs use grades as flavor or quality indicators. Most coffee regions use grading terms to indicate size. Supremo grade Colombian beans, for example, are larger than Excelsco grade Colombian beans. Also, most grade variables do not assess bean ripeness at picking or other taste-related qualities. Marigogipe describes oversized beans of various origins. Peaberry is not a hybrid but an anomaly, a small, round bean resulting from its twin in the cherry not developing. Some say a peaberry's flavor is more concentrated. Most agree that a peaberry bean's shape results in its roasting differently, and for this reason they are sought.

Organic

For a product to earn United States' organic designation, it must meet standards set by the U.S. Department of Agriculture: Beans must be grown using no synthetic pesticides or other prohibited substances for at least three years and the farm must follow a sustainable crop rotation plan.

Other places around the world have different requirements. In the European Union, for example, organic farming includes, at a minimum, crop rotation, strict limits on chemical synthetic pesticide and fertilizer, prohibition of genetically modified organisms, and fair treatment of animals.

The organic label is of significant interest to a small, but growing segment of consumers and certainly important for the environment. But it's hard for some farmers. It requires certification, which in the United States costs about 300 dollars a year. A coffee farm in a developing country may earn just 1,000 dollars per year. The cost automatically excludes smaller family farms. Also, farms deemed non-organic may use environmentally responsible techniques such as contouring their land that just won't earn them organic certification. Organic certification alone is not a fair litmus test.

Sustainable Farming

Sustainable farming means the farmer has a balanced view toward chemicals, with an eye on the big picture and the long-term use of the land. It usually comprises organic practices, good land contouring, and thoughtful recycling whenever possible. For example, a sustainable farm in Guatemala saves the rinse water it uses to process the beans and pours it over the coffee fields to add nutrients back to the soil, conserving water in the process. Sustainability is difficult to standardize and certify because each farm requires individual, thoughtful accommodations.

Fair Trade

Fair trade generally means that a third party oversees the agreement and interactions between seller and buyer to ensure that the seller—farmers, in coffee's case—earn a fair price. Note that most fair trade organizations only certify cooperatives, not individual farms. But that doesn't mean they don't practice fair business or treat their workers well.

< Raw beans in various shapes and colors. They are often sold labeled as organic or fair trade. Learn what these terms mean.

Direct Trade

This relatively new concept in the coffee industry implies a personal relationship between roaster or coffee buyer (but not consumer) and farmer. It means direct trade coffee roasters must have enough resources to visit farms regularly. Despite its limitations, direct trade is a promising label, increasing the likelihood of good quality coffee.

Bird-Friendly/Shade Grown

Many birds winter in warmer climates—many of which happen to be coffee-producing countries— nesting in plantation trees planted to shade the coffee from too much direct sunlight. These same trees offer birds seasonal habitat. So bird-friendly coffee benefits coffee flavor and birds. It also means certification that a farm uses no synthetic chemicals. The cost of this certification is yield; a bird-friendly farm yields approximately one-third less per year.

Lack of such a label does not automatically mean the coffee is unfriendly to birds or of poorer quality. There are other ways to shade coffee trees besides trees. Mountainsides offer similar shade benefits, and some geographic regions feature natural cloud cover. So although being bird-friendly is generally favorable, it's not a conclusive quality indicator.

Q-Grading

While the environment and worker treatment are noble causes, neither directly addresses coffee's number one attraction: flavor. In the U.S., the Specialty Coffee Association of America's Coffee Quality Institute is trying to establish a different standard for grading and trading coffee. The quality part of Q-grading includes an 80 point rating system. Q-grading is a step forward for coffee quality as the industry attempts to find a single label that consumers can use to find good quality and sustainable and fair labor practices in their beans.

Estate Coffee

Estate has replaced the term *plantation* (which has a negative connotation) in this phrase, though no legal definition applies. At best, it means production by a single farm. The right farm uses careful, consistent growing, picking, and processing methods. Potentially, some of the best and most unique coffees come from individual farms. But use of this term provides no real information about what to expect from the product.

Dry/Wet Processed Coffee

How beans get processed matters to the coffee's overall taste outcome. Two methods, dry and wet processing, dominate the coffee industry. For a lengthy discussion of processing, see chapter 2.

Worldwide Guide to Coffee

Now that you know about coffee's history and process, let's talk about its origin—how most of the top Arabica coffee is sold. Origin refers simply to where the coffee was grown. In a general sense, this provides a snapshot of what to expect from the beans. A single-origin coffee comes from one particular country or region. It is not a blend. Each region or country produces coffee with a distinct flavor profile. (The proliferation of micro-businesses that link farms directly to consumers has changed that somewhat, mostly for the better.)

General conditions such as climate and soil contribute to a region's distinct flavor profile. Also, a region's farmers typically use one general farming method. But for all regions, individual farms and microclimates vary. Each region has many flavors across its expanse.

Central and South America

Central and South America produce what many consider the modern coffee taste, despite being the last part of the world to receive and start growing the plant. Coffee producers from this part of the world invented or perfected many modernization techniques.

Brazil

Java may have invented industrialized coffee (see "Java" entry), but Brazil upped the ante. Efficient, flat lands, good climate, and water availability make it the world's coffee king. Though little of its coffee is truly distinctive, there's much to like about it. Because of its notoriously low acidity, this coffee is perhaps the most useful for blending.

Throughout the 1800s and into the early twentieth century, Brazil produced more than half of the world's coffee. In fact, during the second half of the 1800s, Brazil considered recruiting workers from China because its fertile soil returned crops faster than its own population could harvest them. Eventually, Brazil's industry became the first modern mechanized virtual "factory" and invested in infrastructure such as railroad lines to ship coffee.

Brazil's farmers use a variety of processes (though most Brazilian coffee is processed wet) and the country has a variety of climates, but a naturally fertile terroir exists throughout.

Colombia

Before 1900, Colombia didn't grow coffee. By 1940, it had started to compete head-to-head with Brazil, a coffee-growing factory farm that delivered good but not great coffee (see "Brazil" entry above). It was as if the developers were thinking that if Brazil's natural coffee-growing conditions were good, Colombia's were even better.

Colombia developed a standardized system that separated and graded coffees grown on individual farms primarily by size. The system was great for flavor consistency—it practically established a single flavor profile known as Colombian coffee—but nearly eliminated individual farm terroir experiences. In other words, consumers took notice of the "100% Colombian" label but stopped tasting what individual farms could produce. A mass marking campaign surrounding Colombia's fictional folk hero, Juan Valdez, further pushed this notion.

In the past decade, the country's industry has loosened up. It now produces prize-winning varieties from different regions (no more single taste stereotype). Today, this country's coffees are wine-like, balanced with good body, and enjoyed the world over.

Costa Rica

This country's coffee crop has a reputation for having everything, including balance. The terroir contains rich volcanic soil, the weather is ideal for coffee growing, the altitude is high, and the processing is modern. As of this writing, the government also is stable.

What Costa Rican coffee can seem to lack is distinction. Some critics claim it can taste bland even with all essential elements present and in balance—despite being the modern coffee world's model for specialty coffee (meaning it is grown and processed for flavor). Most of its coffee is Caturra, treated with wet processing.

Cuba

No one smuggles Cuban coffee like they do cigars. Cuba is known for coffee, but it is for its brewing preparation rather than taste, which is bland, slightly acidic, and with less than average body. It is usually dark roasted to increase its power. Whether improved farming methods will change this is anyone's guess.

El Salvador

El Salvador coffee, once lost in the world coffee market, is today much more accessible due to availability of small farm lots in the country. El Salvador's farmers produce excellent Arabica Bourbon. The beans have a yellow cast and an unusually sweet smell. This coffee is best used in blends, though the best El Salvador coffee can hold its own as a single origin. Harvest season in El Salvador is late spring, so look for this coffee in June and July.

Guatemala

Guatemala might be considered the Sumatra of Latin America, with plenty of volcanic earth and sun, mountains to prevent overexposure, and a unique wood-burning drying method. It has more Bourbon growths than many of this region's countries, and its beans can typically roast over a wide range. If buying green, roast light and then go darker. Six Guatemalan regions produce unique coffees, perhaps the best known being Antigua, Coban, and Huehuetenango.

Honduras

Honduras produces mostly commodity-grade blend coffees. Honduras's generally low altitude does not preclude good coffee but makes it less likely. Pests enjoy coffee grown at lower elevations, making coffee grown in Honduras more susceptible to infestation.

< A beautiful sight to behold—the well-managed coffee farm.

Jamaica

Jamaica Blue Mountain is among the most expensive beans, akin to Hawaiian Kona. Like Kona, it is memorable when it's good, with the body of a good Sumatran, the bright acidity of the best Kenyan, and the balance of a Costa Rican or Colombian. Jamaica enjoys quite volcanic soil and some farms still use traditional harvesting methods.

When purchasing Jamaican coffee, ask questions. Avoid blends not cost-competitive with other coffees. Most Jamaican coffee is roasted fairly light to preserve its acidity and varietal character. If buying green, don't roast darker than Full City (for more on roast type, see chapter 3, "Coffee Roasts and Roasting").

Mexico

The marketplace undervalues Mexico's coffee, partially because it hasn't been extensively marketed. Mexico has some fine coffees, with nutty brightness, light but pleasant body, snappy acidity, and good balance. With less-than-desirable growing conditions, Mexican farmers must use superior farming methods. Mexican micro-farms have produced some surprises, such as a dry-processed Chiapas from the same-named region. Coatepec, a town in the state of Veracruz, produces one of the best high-grown Mexican coffees.

Nicaragua

Previously unknown or sold as Guatemalan or Costa Rican coffee, Nicaraguan coffee has only recently gained traction. Due to political differences, it was unavailable in parts of the world for some time, including the United States in the 1980s. Nicaraguan farmers produce some fine Bourbon Arabica, generally akin to Guatemalan in taste and appearance, though less smoky.

Peru

Peru is known for filler coffees of little distinction, but has some emerging fine beans, mostly grown on its small family farms. Most Peruvian beans are void of all petrochemical fertilizers and pesticides. Expect good acidity but light body.

Puerto Rico

Until recently, only locals consumed Puerto Rican coffee, minus the country's small annual gift to the Vatican. Puerto Rico has recently attempted to market more but has not gained much traction, perhaps because its coffee is still evolving.

Venezuela

Venezuela, once a significant coffee supplier, has receded over time, starting in the 1980s (possibly due to political instability). Some in the industry speculate that Venezuelan coffee still finds its way to the world marketplace—under the Colombian nameplate. Most of what's available has the typical South American acidity and medium-to-low body.

Asia

Aside from the two countries profiled, the lack of small, upscale farms and craft farmers in this region has prevented a fair assessment Asia's coffee capability or a rough guide to taste.

China

In the late 1800s, French Jesuits brought Bourbon trees to China. During the adventurous 1920s, Shanghai's thriving coffeehouse culture, run mostly by foreigners, catered to Jazz age world travelers. Today, China is a sleeping coffee giant. It's certainly

> Tasting/cupping in coffee-producing countries is becoming more common, which is a good thing. This has not always been the case. Can you imagine a winery where the wine isn't tasted before shipping?

not currently known for coffee. Yet its climate and soil conditions could support a significant bean output. It has a large motivated work force and demonstrated patience (crucial for a farmer). As of publication, a few market experiments were in the works.

To date, tastings have proven good, but short of great or distinctive, with a bland Pacific rim taste. It is full-bodied, but with little of the acidity and/or volcanic richness that makes other regional favorites stars. Currently, the best comes from Yunnan, in southwestern China.

India

No question India is best known for tea. But it has unique climate and farming conditions for its relatively low altitude, creating interesting coffee. India has produced coffee since 1820 when refugees from the Philippines established plantations in Bengal. Some say the plant was planted earlier in Mysore. Indian coffee became popular because of similarities to once-revered Ceylon coffee. Unlike Ceylon, India escaped the devastating leaf rust and root disease of the late nineteenth century.

Indian coffee typically has good body and acidity and can take a wide range of roasts. It is a good choice for single-origin espresso and the secret ingredient in more than one espresso blend.

Java

Javan coffee used to be the large-scale Asian price alternative to Yemen coffee. Dutch colonists built plantations in the 1700s and transplanted Yemen Bourbon trees into the rich Java soil. Java was perfect for growing coffee. Its high moisture provided a humidor-like climate that offered a different, complementary taste profile.

In the late 1860s, two diseases killed off most of Java's Arabica. Javan farmers replanted, mostly with Robusta, and the region has never fully recovered. Today, great Javan coffees are possible but unlikely. Instead, people go to Sumatran (see "Sumatra" entry below).

Javan (and Sumatran) beans are larger than average and have a unique dark, yellowish brown shade. Mocha Java, the original blend, is one-third Yemen Mocha and two-thirds less-costly Java (or Sumatran, often labeled Java).

SPICED COFFEE?

Indian coffee is sometimes grown, stored, and shipped alongside pungent spices such as cinnamon, cardamom, and cloves. Some buyers claim the scents from those crops add flavor notes to the coffees. Though India has some great coffees, much of its crop goes to blending.

Southeast Asia

Southeast Asia, with their focus on commodity coffee, has gone head to head with Brazil in an attempt to unseat them as the leader of large-scale coffee farming. Time will tell if the specialty beans will grow here as they do in Brazil.

Burma

Burma grows a tiny, yet significant amount of coffee called Myanmar. So far, it is only available in northern Europe and Japan, but it may end up in other markets.

Laos

Laos produces Liberica, a rare commodity coffee said to make a distinctive espresso coffee. It can take a variety of roasts. Laotian coffee is difficult to find, although on occasion, a smattering goes to home roasters via online auctioneers.

Vietnam

Vietnam produces a huge amount of commodity coffee but no specialty coffee. The vast majority of its crop is Robusta, no doubt a strategic decision to capitalize on its position behind Brazil as the second largest coffee producer.

Indonesia and Oceania

Indonesian coffees are generally big-boned, flavorful coffees with huge body and a subtle acidity. Even the beans themselves can be oversized. These coffees may be best defined as big but never bland.

Hawaii

Hawaii has great volcanic soil, but historically Hawaiians placed more importance on sugar plantations. To the United States, sugar cane was a worthier investment than coffee.

Sumatra coffee trees amidst taller shade trees.

Hawaii has a good climate and volcanic soil. There is some fine coffee grown there. But, demand is so high that in the 1990s a scandal rocked the coffee world involving coffee imported from Costa Rica that was simply re-labeled Kona.

There isn't enough great Kona. Its wine flavor rivals the best Kenyan, and its subterranean body approaches the best Jamaican Blue Mountain.

If buying for roasting, start light and go just deep enough to Full City. Roast any darker and you'll lose the acidity. Use the same advice for buying Kona, although most pure Kona is roasted fairly light.

Sumatra

A high-humidity climate, volcanic soil, and dated ancient processing methods make Sumatra one of the most satisfying coffees. It has historically been underrated. Sumatran coffee was once sold as Javan, and the best Javan grade at that. Most of the finest Mocha-Java blends were likely Sumatran coffee as well. The gap widened even further when a leaf rust disease destroyed most good Javan coffee but skipped Sumatra altogether.

Expect a good to colossal body. At its best, Sumatran coffee also has a muted spicy acidity that lingers at the back of the mouth. Mandheling and Lintong are two famous districts. The original vintage Sumatra taste depends on dry processing, though some wet processed coffees have the same profile. If buying green to roast, don't over-roast.

Sumatra Variant: Kopi

This famous Sumatra coffee is fed to an Indonesian mammal called a civet and retrieved post-digestion. Despite its source, Kopi coffee is quite good, but it's expensive. If you get the chance, try Kopi. You'll be surprised by its body and acidity.

Sulawesi

In a quick taste snapshot, Sulawesi appears a refined Sumatran with more acidity, less body, and a cleaner, if sometimes less distinctive taste.

Sulawesi seems a more consistent coffee than Sumatran. Whether this is due to farming practices, processing, industry, climate, or other conditions is unknown, but many in the industry say they buy Sulawesi coffees with more assurance than Sumatrans. A noted coffee shop owner once said, "Sulawesi coffee is Sumatra coffee with all its problems fixed."

Sulawesi is often labeled Celebes, which is not a region but actually the island's original name. Reportedly, the best Sulawesi coffee comes from Toraja, a mountain in the island's center.

Papua New Guinea

If Sulawesi is a refined Sumatran, Papua New Guinea might be considered a refined Sulawesi.

MOCHA DISTINCTIONS

Mocha is one of the coffee world's most commonly used words. It denotes beans grown in Yemen. Sometimes, neighboring Ethiopian (and even Brazilian) beans receive the Mocha label, an inaccuracy dating from coffee's casual labeling history. Today, the term also describes chocolate, hence its use to describe an espresso beverage made with chocolate flavoring, and a European mildly pressurized drip method. The latter is spelled Moka.

It has the highest acidity of the Indonesian coffees. The balance definitely tilts upward, meaning more pronounced acidity than body—a rarity for Pacific coffees. The region generally practices wet processing, though some farms dry process.

Yemen

Yemen coffee causes endless arguments among coffee connoisseurs. It is old and its coffee-growing culture breaks all the rules, yet it is still revered as one of the best varieties. It is grown almost at sea level and is almost all dry processed, irregularly and often sloppily. The beans all look different and have a decidedly ragged appearance. It's part of the processing and not necessarily indicative of a quality problem.

But amidst the broken beans, insect damage, mold, and other artifacts, the coffee displays so much flavor balance and complexity that it is easy to taste why Yemen's coffee business flourishes. If you want perfectly shaped, even-colored beans, don't try Yemen coffee. But if it's taste you want, the small irregular beans provide coffee unlike any other.

Yemen is all Bourbon and almost certainly organic, although it is rarely certified. Good beans come from all over Yemen, with much of it from the country's cottage industry, grown on small plots behind houses and dried on rooftops. It blends perfectly with Javan or Sumatran coffee.

When buying green, expect less-than-perfect appearance. Resist the urge to over-roast to create a more uniform appearance. If buying roasted, don't be afraid of a less-than-uniform looks. The best tasting Yemen Mocha can look uneven and be roasted light. Yemen will also take a dark roast and is overall a flexible coffee.

>
This coffee is sorted by hand, an important step in quality control.

Africa

The African continent's coffees are definitive; anything else is a variation. African coffees tend to be wine-like, with good but not overly present bodies. Some of the world's smallest beans come from Africa, but they have intensely concentrated flavor.

Democratic Republic of the Congo (DRC)

The DRC (formerly Zaire) produces some fine coffees, but they are not widely available so the country has little name recognition.

Ethiopia

This widely accepted coffee birthplace has a long, mostly unblemished history. The commodity coffee trade brought the bean to other countries, where factory plantation methods ruined it. But Ethiopia kept its fine growing and processing traditions.

Dry processing creates the best Ethiopian coffees. The coffee, typically full-bodied with a light fruitiness, exhibits two main taste footprints called Harrar and Sidamo/Yirga Chefe. Harrar has a cleaner taste, a lighter body, and a decided blueberry note. Sidamo is spicy. Yirga Chefe, a city within Sidamo province, markets its coffee by its town name (the only noticeable difference between Yirga Chefe and Sidamo).

Ethiopian coffee is inconsistent. Labeling problems make it frustrating to find the same coffee flavor twice. If you come across one you like, grab it. If roasting, err on the side of light roasts.

Kenya

Kenyan is the most famous non-Arab African coffee. The country also has one of the world's most modern coffee industries, probably because it planted coffee late. It was the first coffee country to adopt a reasonable grading system that addresses coffee quality. Kenya AA is the highest. The best Kenyan coffee comes from Mount Kenya.

All Kenyan coffees are wet-processed and most likely Caturra. Kenyan coffee is wine-like and full bodied, but it's distinctive with unique blackberry notes.

Rwanda

Rwandan coffee has a high acidity and full body. Though Rwandan coffee is known for being washed, its dry-processed versions (though rare) are stellar.

Tanzania

Tanzanian coffee, which grows on Mounts Kilimanjaro and Meru, tastes much like a good Kenyan, with the same African wine-like footprint. Some Tanzanian coffees taste like Ethiopian coffee.

Uganda

Uganda has created some great coffee on mountains near Kenya, but the country does not produce large quantities. That it does produce gets lost in the mainstream specialty business. If roasting, don't roast too far.

Zimbabwe

Zimbabwean coffee has little name recognition, though it offers a rich body and nice balance. It has the same winey acidity as a Kenyan, without the blackberry note. Even so, more than one commercial coffee roasting company has labeled Zimbabwean coffee Kenyan to sell it at a higher price. Some of the best Zimbabwean coffee comes from the town of Chipinge under a Salimba label.

Additional Coffee-Buying Considerations

The coffee world is changing. Even the most careful listing of regions and coffees won't offer you an exact roadmap. Thanks to direct trade, the World Wide Web, and small family farms, we now have much greater access to high-quality coffees that defy categorization.

When choosing a variety, ask yourself these questions:

1 How does it smell? If it's green and for roasting, how fresh is it?

2. What genus of bean is it?

3. Is it from a small farm? Does my coffee buyer know anything about the farm's methods?

Pay less attention to whether it's organic, bird-friendly/shade grown, or fair-traded (unless it's commodity coffee).

The rubber meets the road in the coffee seller's shop. Use varieties as a starting point. But before simply deciding based on geography, ask questions. It's better to buy a great coffee from an unknown or underappreciated region (e.g., Nicaragua) than a mediocre coffee from a well-known one (e.g., Sumatra). Most regional differences are wider ranging than even coffee buyers assume. I have tasted great coffee from almost every world region and country. If I haven't, I assume it's because I have not run into it yet. I never rule out new varieties. Neither should you.

Taste Comes First

I know I may get flak for downplaying environmental sustainability and labor issues. I agree with these goals in spirit, but I sincerely believe that any product sold primarily for taste must taste good first. With coffee, aroma comes in a close second. In fact, you almost can't separate coffee's taste and aroma. Fortunately, most environmental, sustainability, and labor issues lead to good-flavored coffee.

Also, geography isn't everything. It is important to understand geographic coffee-growing regions because so much of flavor depends on terroir. But the increase of micro-lots farmed and processed by individuals complicates the equation. For example, a farm in Honduras recently began selling coffee from plant cuttings brought from Ethiopia. Startlingly, this coffee tastes more Ethiopian than other Honduran coffees. Is the earth less important than previously assumed?

Where the bean originated still carries authority when predicting taste. The most important decision when taking a photograph is choosing a worthy subject. In the case of coffee beans, the first step is finding beans worth turning into coffee.

2 SELECTING COFFEE BEANS

IN CHAPTER 1 we learned that although most commercial coffee sells as branded blends from the beans of many countries, upscale coffee tends to have a single country of origin (such as Guatemala or Ethiopia). The higher the price and the more unique the taste, the greater the likelihood of regions within a country (such as Sumatra's Mandheling) or individual estates or farms (such as Costa Rica's La Manita) selling their own coffee.

Thanks to Internet commerce and global shipping, it is conceivable that someone in the United States could purchase online a single-origin coffee grown on a plot in the Guatemalan mountains. Just a short time ago, such point-to-point individuality and identity tracking could only be imagined.

For practical purposes, we devote this chapter to bean freshness. By the end, you will know how to do the following:

- Identify and evaluate the best, freshest coffees, and choose the best one for you

- Taste coffee

- Differentiate blends and formulate your own personal blend

- Host a coffee cupping

< Top: roasted coffee beans; bottom: green, unroasted coffee beans.
Beans generally swell in size and lose weight when roasted.

Coffee Characteristics

Coffee is such a delicate fruit that almost any difference in where and how it's grown, picked, graded, sorted, processed, packaged, and shipped—even its botanical DNA—seems to make a marked difference in how it tastes in your cup. Understanding these differences is essential for learning how to choose the best beans, whether already roasted or those you plan to roast yourself.

Species

Several coffee plant species fall under the Rubiaceae family, genus name *Coffea*. Arabica is the original cultivated plant species and the one that offers the finest potential flavor. Two others, Robusta and Liberica, are used commercially but primarily in commodity coffee. (See chapter 1, "Knowing Your Coffee Beans," page 11 for a complete list of species, subspecies, and descriptions.)

Terroir

The earth in which the coffee trees are planted makes a big difference in a bean's flavor. As gardeners know, soil feeds the plants, so coffee grown in different soil absorbs different nutrients. (It is similar to how grain-fed chicken or grass-fed cattle produce meat with different flavors than their commercial counterparts.) Jamaica's rich volcanic soil produces different tasting coffee than chalky or sandy Yemen soils even if the beans come from the same parent trees.

Climate

Rainfall, sunlight, temperature, and other environmental factors all affect how beans grow and taste. A region's particular climate influences season length, speed of bean-ripening, and water's role as a nutrient. For example, coffee grown in thinner mountain air ripens later. Cloudy skies, tall trees, and mountains each form a canopy that protects beans from harsh sunlight.

Farming Standards

A number of farming techniques nurture coffee beans into realizing their full potential. Soil fertilization, pruning, watering, and other tree care change the soil's ability to feed the trees. For example, contoured soil ensures equal distribution of water among trees.

Farmers must harvest beans at their peak ripeness to ensure a top-quality crop. This means picking coffee several times during the month so that beans are ripe. A single picking means some beans will be under-ripe; others will be over-ripe. Harvesting a tree's beans en masse—ripe, under-ripe, and all—compromises the coffee's quality. Also, coffee trees only produce quality beans through so many harvests, meaning a properly managed farm replants its trees regularly.

Beloved Sumatra cherries and green beans, side by side.

Processing

The fruit of the coffee tree looks much like cherries—round and fleshy with a large seed pit. To make coffee, these seeds must be removed from the trees and dried. How and how well this happens affects flavor. There are two methods of processing: dry and wet.

Dry processing is the original method still practiced in many regions worldwide, particularly near coffee's Ethiopian birthplace. In this process, picked cherries dry out on a sun-exposed surface, such as a flat rooftop, causing the skin and fruit to become brittle and easy to remove. Layering beans is fine, as long as they get turned regularly to avoid scorched top layers and moldy bottom layers. Skin removal requires skill and good judgment; if too much skin gets peeled, the beans lose a layer of protection, potentially allowing premature staleness or mold. Most, if not all, of the dry process happens by hand.

The dry process likely presents the purest representation of a coffee bean and its terroir, offering nothing but the bean's flavor as nature grew it. Dry processing also offers more viscosity, mouth feel, body, depth, muted acidity, and potentially earthy flavors, and it requires less water—particularly important in climates with barely enough for human consumption. But the process is quite time-consuming and labor-intensive.

In wet processing, coffee cherries soften in large vats of water. A machine then mechanically removes the seeds: the soft fruit peels away and floats as the seeds (beans) sink to the bottom. The flesh gets discarded or composted. The seeds are then dried using either the natural, old-fashioned sun method or in mechanical dryers. With the latter, beans can dry out too much if not watched carefully, and then cracking can make them vulnerable to mold formation. Once dried, they are hulled, mechanically or by hand, and the skins removed not much past the outer protective coating.

Wet processing offers brighter acidity and an arguably cleaner, less earthy taste due to quicker skin removal. But it involves water, adding the risk of mold formation.

Storage and Shipping

Coffee beans are like sponges that easily pick up off-tastes and odors. Climate during transit and warehousing also affect flavor. For example, beans stored in high humidity can ferment or rot. Beans stored in any environment for an extended period lose flavor.

Beans have long been shipped in sacks made of jute (or burlap), which are economical and practical for handling but expose beans to moisture, air, and odors during their shipping. Water shipment, still the standard coffee bean transport method, means long sea voyages, exposure to moisture for extended periods of time, and storage next to all manner of products, some inert and others not. Once a shipment of coffee arrives in port, it can get damaged if not properly stored.

Roast

Different roasts make otherwise identical beans taste completely different. Roasting is such an essential, complex component of a bean's flavor that we've devoted chapter 3 entirely to it.

An assortment of raw green coffee beans ready for roasting.

Green Coffee Bean Basics

In a perfect world, the best coffee beans grow in rich earth, protected from harsh sunlight, and get picked by farmers who choose the exact moment of ripeness, carefully remove the beans, and then ship them to us. Or would that actually be perfect? For every common-sense agricultural rule, there's a coffee example to defy it. Those rule-breaking coffees are often among the finest.

Take Yemen Mocha, for example. Often, the coffee cherries appear as dry as raisins while growing. They receive far too much sunlight and Yemen's arid climate robs them of any but an occasional

watering. They grow practically at sea level, a far cry from choice high-altitude mountains. They dry on rooftops, mostly because farmers there are far too poor and live in such a water-scarce region that they cannot consider using even the most primitive water hull-removal equipment.

So are there no rules? The best we have are centuries' worth of trials and errors from each region. Though not hard and fast, the tips that follow at least provide some quality predictors to make us better buyers.

Buying Beans in Season

Coffee flavor is a constantly moving target. Like a flower, coffee can lose its scent seemingly in an instant. To make sure the coffee tastes its best, use it quickly. That means drinking what's in season, which requires knowing when various coffee-growing regions plant and harvest their crops.

Think about what season it is right now. Like most crops, coffee requires time from its initial budding until the beans ripen for harvesting. Some countries such as Guatemala have just one annual harvest because of their dramatic wet and dry seasons. Others with more consistent climates such as Ethiopia harvest multiple times throughout the year. A country such as Brazil, with its giant, industrial approach to coffee and consistent weather, harvests year-round. Most countries have one or two harvests annually.

Within a given region, not all beans ripen simultaneously. One farm at higher altitude that experiences dry conditions may harvest its coffee a month later than others in the area. The beans on a farm with greater sun exposure may ripen earlier than one shaded by trees or a mountain. Often, the earlier ripening and picked coffees are lower quality. In the coffee industry, here's the rule of thumb: Middle-arriving beans are the best. Of course, as in all things coffee, there's an asterisk. Coffee pickers, typically paid by their yield and not for their discernment, may pick unripe or past-prime cherries to earn more money. Beans are simply more plentiful at the early and late stages of the season.

Green coffee, like roasted coffee, can go stale. So regardless of harvest time quality range, it's wise to buy green coffees six weeks after harvest to allow for processing and shipment. Beans available earlier, sometimes called new crop beans, likely come from the lowest elevation. Coffees bought late in the season may have lost flavor, either from over-ripeness, inadequate or improper storage before processing, or flavor loss due to warehousing after processing. Exceptions to this are the so-called aged coffees, green beans specially stored in climate-controlled conditions so they can soften, or lose acidity.

Once you purchase green beans, you have a second roughly six-week window to roast them at their peak.

AGING GRACEFULLY

When properly controlled and when used in blends or as single origins, the aged effect offers qualities prized by the coffee connoisseur. However, I caution the novice who attempts to purchase aged coffee. It's a fine line line between aged and old. The allure of green beans labeled "aged" has fooled even the most veteran coffee buyers.

Colombia, Venezuela, Sumatra, Java, and India sometimes offer aged coffees. India's Monsoon Malabar is named for its storage through the monsoon season, which reportedly subjects it to unusual conditions and creates a strong flavor you either love or hate.

Global Coffee Harvests

This chart lists several coffee-growing regions and their harvest times, followed by approximate dates for shipping each season's coffee crop. Most of the Northern Hemisphere's peak harvest time is between December and March. Most of the Southern Hemisphere's peak harvest time is from May through September. (6–8 weeks shipping time implies market availability.)

REGION/COUNTRY	HARVEST/PROCESSING	SHIPPING/BEST TIME TO BUY
Americas		
Brazil	May–August	July–May
Colombia	September–January	March–June
Costa Rica, Guatemala	October–March	December–July
Honduras	October–February	December–May
Mexico	October–March	December–May
Nicaragua	December–March	December–July
Panama	November–March	December–June
El Salvador	November–March	December–July
Venezuela	October–February	October–March
India	December–March	January–June
Papua New Guinea	May–August	July–December
Hawaii	November–March	November–August
INDONESIA		
Java	June–October	July–December
Sulawesi (formerly Celebes) Kalossie	May–November	July–December
Sumatra	October–March	November–June
Timor	June–September	July–December
AFRICA		
Democratic Republic of the Congo	January–April	May–June
Ethiopia, Tanzania	November–February	December–June
Uganda	October–January	October–January
Yemen	October–December	December–April
Zimbabwe	July–September	October–March
CARRIBEAN		
Jamaica	January–March	January
Dominican Republic	November–April	December–July

Buying Fresh Roasted Beans

Where can you buy green beans? Before the 1990s, consumers couldn't. Commercial green brokers almost never sold direct to consumers, and those who did often sold them by 150-pound (68 kg) bags. Consumers who approached local commercial roasting companies met perplexed, even offended, roast masters who acted like a restaurant chef asked to sell a steak for someone to cook at home.

The Internet changed all of this, making it possible to find online sources for beans at a range of prices and sizes. Not sure where to start online? Search for award-winning green beans. Buy a few pounds (enough to last awhile and make shipping economical but not so much that you're stuck if you don't enjoy it). And remember that you want to use them while they're still fresh. That's the whole idea. Sign up for home roast coffee forums and become active. Word of mouth is a good way to find the good stuff. You know you've arrived when you find yourself setting an alarm for 2:00 AM so you can bid on some Kenya AA "Best of Cup" award-winning lots. Then you'll know the real reason for caffeine. For specific places to buy green coffee online, see the "Resources" section in the back of the book, starting on page 168.

When buying already-roasted coffee beans, someone else chose the green beans and presumably followed the guidelines we just discussed. Make sure you check the roast (which we cover in chapter 3, "Coffee Roasts and Roasting") because a coffee's roast is crucial to its taste. So are its bean and roast freshness.

Beans are at their fresh flavor peak one to fourteen days following roasting. The first twenty-four hours after roasting is called resting. During this period, coffees typically are too fresh to be at their best. A coffee brewed immediately after roasting will foam up when hot water hits the grounds in the brewer due to excessive carbon dioxide escaping from the beans and impeding the extraction process (see "Brewing," chapter 5). Truthfully, this is rarely a problem when buying already-roasted beans.

You want fresh beans whenever possible. The best way to buy fresh is to find a shop that roasts its own beans or roasts locally and receives regular deliveries. If you buy coffee anywhere else, how it's packaged becomes important. Here are some freshness guidelines.

- Look at the label. Labels on fresh-roasted coffee beans should list their roast date. Beans should be used within two weeks of roasting, so be suspicious of a date more than two weeks prior.

- Ask questions. For coffee beans packaged without a freshness date, ask when the roasting happened. "This morning," "Yesterday," or even "Last week" are good answers. You don't want to hear "This past spring" or "No idea."

- Be wary of "Best by" dates. Some coffee roasting companies project their products' freshness will last up to a year. Try to use this date to calculate the date of bean roasting.

- Seek out beans packaged in methods that prolong freshness. For example, one-way valve bags allow air to exit but do not allow air inside. Also, beans packaged while surrounded by nitrogen don't stale as quickly because little oxygen enters the bag.

- Consider aroma (does it smell right?), storage (where and how is the coffee stored?) and turnover (how quickly does the store sell its stock?) when trying to find fresh beans.

Freezing Coffee Beans

Freezing coffee beans or grounds is controversial in the coffee industry. Adherents claim it prolongs freshness. Detractors claim coffee oils and aromas inside the beans cannot literally be frozen and that the condensation that forms on the beans as they go in and come out of the freezer cancels out any improvements. After many years of testing and analysis, I believe that freezing beans or grounds works well to give them additional shelf life—as long as they are appropriately packaged and removed.

Two innovations appear to greatly slow the green coffee-staling process: airtight containment and bean freezing. Airtight and opaque materials such as aluminum foil—not, at first glance, innovative but radically different technology in the world of coffee—block oxygen, moisture, and competing aromas. This allows for bean shipment alongside other products without concern that outside scents or moisture will damage the coffee. Tests conducted by a major U.S. importer have shown that aluminum barrier packaging results in beans with fewer off-tastes and less moisture damage.

Also keep roasted beans—those you roast at home or those you purchase already-roasted—fresh by freezing them. Freeze beans roasted at home immediately after cooling. Freeze already-roasted beans immediately after purchase. Say your favorite Internet roasting company offers free shipping with a three-pound (1.4 kg) bean purchase. Here's what I would do:

1. Freeze a maximum of one-third of the package (or one week's worth of beans) per container. If separated into three, keep the coffee in the packages in which it came. Leave one at room temperature for use.

2. Cover each bean bag you plan to freeze with a second freezer bag.

3. Squeeze out the air and seal tightly. Freeze.

4. Each time you remove a coffee bag from the freezer, let it come to room temperature before opening its outer bag or original package.

5. Once at room temperature, unseal package and use as you would fresh-roasted beans. Keep it tightly closed and set it away from bright light in a cool place, away from heat.

6. Do not refreeze.

Some hobbyists divide their beans into coffee pot–sized portions before freezing. This way, they can remove just enough to brew one pot without exposing the other beans to air and humidity. Use two bags per serving for double insulation.

Evaluating the Freshness of Roasted Beans

To test for freshness, grind some roasted coffee beans, place them in an open-drip filter, and pour freshly boiled hot water over the grounds. Fresh-roasted coffee will swell up from the release of carbon dioxide gas. Stale coffee will remain flat throughout the brew cycle. Of course, such a test, by its nature, happens too late. We want to know before we buy our beans whether they are fresh.

You can roast green beans to light or dark roasts.

The Basics of Blended Beans

Bean blends combine the best qualities of one single origin with the different but complementary qualities of another, resulting in a unique, signature taste. In a perfect blend, the result is greater than the individual parts, causing a third unique flavor to emerge. Sometimes the word "distinguished" describes this signature taste.

Blending experts typically combine no more than three different coffees. Many commercial blends feature more than three coffee varieties, but this is mostly due to practical considerations such as bean sourcing and availability. Keep in mind, a large roasting company needs to distribute a large volume of coffee and once it promotes a blend needs to maintain its flavor consistency and cost.

The home aficionado has no such constraints. We can create a one-time perfect blend that we never have to recreate or mass produce. We likely care little if the varieties we blend are expensive. We aim to create unique, personal flavors. Leave consistency to others.

Starting from scratch on your own blend can be a challenge. Here are three examples of proven blends to give you a taste:

- Mocha-Java: One-third Yemen Mocha to two-thirds Sumatra Mandheling, all Full City roast

- Black and Tan: One-half Vienna Roast (dark roast) Colombian to one-half City roast (light roast) Colombian

- Proprietary Roast #1: One-quarter Kenya AA to one-quarter Guatemala Coban to one-half Brazil, all Full City roast

Crafting a Personal Bean Blend

To start crafting your personal blend, combine two varieties of brewed coffee you enjoy and see how they taste together. Use a yin/yang approach. For example, try pairing a bright Colombian coffee with a low-acid Brazilian coffee. Many types of satisfying combinations exist. Check out chapter 1 for a list of regional traits. It's a good place to create your short list. (It's best to experiment using brewed coffee rather than beans. Then it becomes a matter of recreating that same ratio using coffee beans.)

Tweak your blend by changing the percentages of each coffee variety, or try blending half light roast and half dark roast of any two coffees, even two of the same variety. It's a trade secret that one well-regarded specialty blend is actually a single-origin variety made from two roasts from two different Colombian bean regions.

Materials

Brewed coffee samples of each potential blend component

Coffee brewer (pick your favorite from chapter 5, "Brewing," and follow instructions)

Thermal carafe for each brewed sample, to keep coffee hot

8-ounce (240 ml) measuring cup (one for each coffee)

Coffee cups or drinking vessels

Instructions

1. Brew each coffee sample and then pour each into a thermos to preserve heat.

2. Measure 5 ounces (150 ml) of each into individual measuring cups. Pour 3 ounces (90 ml) of one into a coffee cup and then add 1 ounce (30 ml) of another to the same cup.

3. Repeat, sampling until you reach your desired ratio.

4. When you get a cup you like, note its ratios.

5. Finally, mix roasted beans in identical portions. This should allow you to streamline future production runs of your blend by roasting the beans blended. Note, however, that several industry roast masters claim their blends must be roasted one variety at a time and that size, moisture, and other differences between their blends' varieties change the flavors when roasted together.

Cupping

Coffee cupping is the process to evaluate coffee's taste, the stop-and-smell-the-roses step in your development as a coffee drinker. Have you ever seen a wine taster swirling a vintage Cabernet in a glass and sniffing it before taking a tiny sip? Well, cupping is the coffee world's equivalent.

And it has layers of flavor. It awakens taste buds on your tongue as it flows around your mouth. Coffee gets more flavorful as it cools. Where wine drinkers credit wine's relaxing qualities for giving its imbibers more taste toward the end of a glass, coffee drinkers cite coffee's stimulating quality as a flavor enhancer. That means the second cup is often tastier than the first.

A classic cupping operation uses tiny ceramic coffee cups, but rocks glasses, china, or glassware suit the technique as well. If cupping with others, you may wish to prepare separate samples for each participant. If you share, rinse your spoon as you cup. People who cup often obtain a special cupping spoon that is wide like a soup spoon, almost round in shape, with a snub nose.

I can't wait any longer. Let's get started.

How to Cup Coffee

Cupping is best done in a relaxed style. It requires a head free of colds or other barriers to smell and taste buds free of strong competing flavors. Ample time is the only practical way to allow for multiple tastings as the coffee cools, so it is important to allot enough time. Allow a minimum of one hour to cup up to six coffees.

Keeping a Journal of How to Cup

A coffee buyer I know has kept a cupping journal for more than forty years. She has recorded impressions of every Sumatra crop since her start in the industry (when women were first allowed into the cupping rooms). She can conjure in great detail the 1982 Mandheling crop. She can spot up and comers and predict future great coffees by tracking which farms are problem solving and developing the best beans. If you don't keep a log, as she says, a cup of coffee lasts only minutes. With a log, your coffee lasts as long as the ink remains on the page.

Materials

Tea kettle

1 6-ounce (180 ml) rocks glass for each coffee sample

1 water glass per participant, for rinsing spoons

3 to 6 fresh ground coffee samples

Scale, to weigh coffees

1 cupping spoon per participant

Log book to score and describe the coffees

1 serving sparkling water for each participant, to cleanse palate between cupping, optional

Spittoon, such as a tall glass or bowl, optional

< A cupping kit is comprised of a kettle, water pitcher, small cups with ground coffee, cupping spoon, and cupping log.

To Spit or Not to Spit?

That is a question for which there is no answer, or rather, the answer is a personal choice. Professional cuppers keep a spittoon nearby. For them, it is necessary because they cup many coffees in a day (and still need to get a full night's sleep). If only cupping a few favorites, I recommend fully enjoying the coffee by drinking it. Always keep a spittoon or other receptacle nearby in case a coffee doesn't taste good. Consider using a large glass, bowl, or other receptacle that you can empty and reuse. Also, sparkling water does wonders for refreshing the palate. Keep a bottle on hand for sipping between cuppings.

Instructions

1. Fill a kettle (you can never have too much hot water) with filtered, good-tasting water and set it to boil on the stove.

2. Set out small glasses, one for each coffee sample. Place a few large water glasses at the center of the arrangement.

3. Place 2 tablespoons (10 g) of fresh finely ground coffee in each rocks glass for each 6-ounce (180 ml) sample **(a)**. The tall water glasses should not have coffee in them.

4. Once the water boils, turn off the burner and wait for 1 minute.

5. Pour 6 ounces (180 ml) of hot water into each cup. Do not stir the grounds. Fill the tall glasses two-thirds of the way with hot water **(b)**. You will rinse your cupping spoons in these glasses, as needed.

6. Allow the coffee to steep for four minutes. Then, with a large cupping spoon, break the crust of grounds on each coffee sample **(c)**. As you do this, place your nose as close as possible to the sample and inhale the coffee's aromas. In your cupping log or a note pad, record your observations.

7. With the spoon, remove and discard the floating pieces of crust from each sample. **(d)** (The wet grounds clump together and are easy to remove.)

8. Rinse the spoon in a hot water bath. Dip the clean spoon into one sample and carefully slurp it into your mouth. The louder the slurp, the more likely you are doing it authentically, as they do in Amsterdam's cupping houses **(e)**.

9. Note the various taste sensations in your cupping log or note pad. Rinse your spoon before moving to a new sample.

10. Taste all the samples, noting all flavors in your cupping log. I know professional cuppers whose logs go back forty years or more.

11. Repeat the slurping as the coffee cools. You may be surprised at the difference in your results. Coffee taste can change dramatically after it cools.

12. Once you have sniffed and tasted all coffees hot, warm, and at room temperature, you are finished.

3 COFFEE ROASTS AND ROASTING

ROASTING is a simple, linear cooking art, yet it is filled with variables that can make dramatic differences in your coffee. Roasting artisans have the process down pat. If you want to control every aspect of coffee enjoyment, roasting at home is the way to go.

Unless you grow your own coffee, which is impossible for most of us, roasting completes the circle of coffee involvement. It's also fun, and perhaps even more than brewing, allows you to witness the alchemy of turning these little fruit seeds called coffee beans into real, sweet-smelling treasure chests filled with aromatic, flavorful oils.

Roasting at home doesn't mean you'll never buy roasted coffee. In fact, you just may develop a new appreciation for the artisans and their roasting prowess. Whether you decide to become your own roast master for life or be just an occasional roaster

who otherwise buys already-roasted coffee beans, you will never forget your first roasting experience.

By the end of this chapter, you will understand the following:

- Distinguishing characteristics of six different roasts

- Pros and cons of and how to use stovetop roasting, drum roasting, and fluid-air roasting

- The process of home roasting and how to determine whether it's right for you

< Hot-air coffee roasters create a hot-air bed that lifts the beans, constantly recirculating them. This method effectively, quickly, and evenly roasts all the beans.

Commercial and Micro-Roasting

Until the 1970s, large commercial roasters, the pinnacle of modernized robotic industrialization, roasted most coffee in the United States. Gas-fired drum roasters supplied the coffee for your supermarkets. An octopus of pipes hosed from large vats of green beans fed the largest machines. Good roasters, even large commercial ones, existed, feeding good quality beans into their goliath roasters. In fact, the majors could (and certainly still can) roast good, high-quality coffee beans. In terms of consistency and ability to monitor and repeat a roast, large-batch roasters are second to none.

But as roasters grew larger, the coffee they produced often seemed to lack something. In the 1970s, a couple of interesting and synergistic events occurred. First, as big roasters roasted larger batches and centralized operations, they required huge green bean lots. This left the smaller farmers' yields unsold. Meanwhile, a new generation of small or micro-roasters (roasting machines that roast five or ten pounds [2.3 or 4.5 kg] at a time) came to market. The mentality started to change, as better, cheaper, point-to-point transportation and other factors allowed a small-roaster operation in Cleveland, for example, to purchase beans directly from a Guatemalan farm.

On top of that, Baby Boomers—people of the "me" generation—were now adults and wanted special products of all kinds to celebrate their individuality and self-indulgence. Their parents sought simplified, generic products for their post-war lives, but Boomers wanted and were willing to pay for quality. That mentality gave birth to the specialty coffee business, with micro-roasting a natural outgrowth of the movement. Small-batch roasters could purchase specialty beans at bargain prices, roast them fresh, and sell them in their new boutique stores or in supermarkets savvy enough to see a market for this alternative to centrally roasted large-batch (mostly) canned coffees. Boomers (and even some older consumers) quickly began to appreciate the attention to quality and freshness of these new micro-roasts.

NOT TOO SCIENTIFIC

All of this may sound science-based, yet little of coffee is scientific compared to other cooking arts. Many people still take into account intuition, superstition, and urban myth when roasting coffee. It makes sense: It's hard to know exactly what happens to coffee beans as they roast.

Take temperature, for example. To know a bean's internal temperature, all you need to do is stick a probe into a bean, right? Not exactly. Remember that beans are hard and brittle, especially as they roast. The best we can measure bean temperature is by inserting a probe into a group of roasting beans, to get a temperature reading at least close to the inside temperature. It's so difficult to know bean temperature that many commercial roasters use visual tryers, removable scoops that catch beans as they roast and allow the roast master to pull a sample to check its status against a visual color tile (see photo at right).

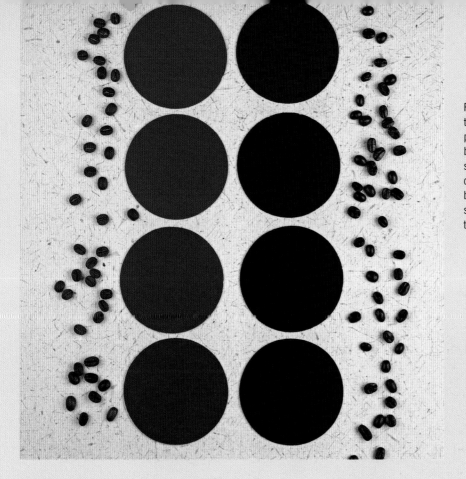

Roast tiles are used to gauge the color of roasted beans. With practice, you can determine a bean's roasting doneness by sight, looking at its lightness/darkness and color, by sound, by its crackling character and speed, and by smell in addition to temperature.

The Science of Roasting

The heat required to roast coffee equals the heat with which people in the industry argue about how to do it. Some adherents use low heat to drive moisture from the beans until pyrolysis, or first crack. Then they finish the beans to the desired roast by increasing heat. Others use high heat early, searing the beans like a steak, then low heat after first crack, as the beans should have a high enough internal temperature to finish by themselves.

Roasting brings raw, green coffee beans to a state called pyrolysis, which generally occurs at from 400°F to 420°F (204°C to 216°C), and liberates about 150 to 200 BTUs (158 to 211 kilojoules) of heat. Roasting has been called the moment of truth because until coffee is roasted, its taste remains unknown.

It takes time to get to pyrolysis. As beans roast, they progress through various stages. At 220°F (104°C), they shrivel up and lose moisture and weight. They then swell to twice their size. At 380°F (197°C), they turn pale brown. At 400°F (204°C), they turn medium brown. During this process, free amino acids react with reducing sugars resulting in more than 110 aromatic compounds. Also, during roasting, the beans lose then gain sugars, and their acidity decreases, then returns to its starting pH level. Light-roasted coffees have lower pH levels. By the time coffee finishes roasting, more than 700 identified compounds—cumulatively called coffee flavor—exist.

Coffee Roasts Defined

There are several standard popular (commercial) coffee roasts. No matter where you buy your beans, whether it's a large, well-known chain or a boutique micro-roastery shop, you should find the same familiar terms. There are some regional variations and some companies have created their own order and names. But this list can serve as a useful guide for the roasts you will most likely encounter.

Cinnamon/New England (1)

This light, popular roast defines coffee found at donut shops and in breakfast nooks. But before you dismiss it as a commodity or supermarket roast, consider that the very best beans from some of the country's highest-end roasters are roasted light. Because this roast is so revealing, even the slightest flavor defect—a sour note that a darker roast might smooth out, for example—becomes apparent.

High acidity, slightly less body than the City roast, and no caramel notes typify this roast, which allows the clearest portrait of an origin's genetic flavor footprint and should sparkle in the cup. Single origins are easiest to identify when roasted to this light roast. A frequent side effect of this roast is less body or mouth feel.

City/Full City (2)

City and Full City roasts are one or two shades deeper and darker than a Cinnamon/New England roast but still have no pronounced roast flavor. The extra roasting time develops sugars and provides caramel notes with little loss of acidity in the best-quality beans. The majority of specialty coffee is roasted to City or Full City roast.

< These roasted bean samples illustrate the range of commonly available roasts. Roast "doneness" is as important an element in your coffee cup as any other factor.

Vienna (3)

Named for the coffeehouses in the famous Austrian metropolis, Vienna roast is just a shade darker than Full City. Visually, you should start to see sweating in the form of tiny oil droplets on still-brown beans. In the mouth, the caramel notes should predominate, though not at the loss of varietal uniqueness. In other words, a Sumatran coffee roasted to a Vienna should still taste like a Sumatran coffee but a very syrupy one.

Espresso (4)

As the name suggests, Espresso roast, which is darker than a Vienna roast, is the most common Italian classic espresso roast. Any lighter roast than this will likely make espresso taste bitter due to the high-pressure extraction method an espresso maker uses, which seems to highlight acidity. This roast, for which beans are often roasted slightly longer and at lower temperatures, has very balanced flavors.

Italian (5)

This roast has more pronounced oil and bittersweet notes, which add complexity at the cost of acidity. Much of the world considers Italian roast the standard espresso roast as it's just slightly darker than the Espresso roast but with more oil spots on the beans' surface.

French (6)

The classic French roast has a pronounced roasted note. It's almost like super-dark bread baked with a dark crust, where you can taste the darkness in every bite. It's beyond caramel. It has spicy charcoal notes, much like food cooked on a grill. Beans roasted French roast are often shiny because their oils have surfaced and coated their exterior.

Home Roasting Techniques

Home roasting has the allure of easy entry. All you need is a hot air corn popper (something many people already have) and the ability to purchase (or talk your local roasting shop into providing) a sample of green beans. Then it's a matter of tossing them into the corn popper and starting the machine. Just like that, you can roast coffee.

One reason few people roast coffee at home for long is cost. Yes, you can purchase green beans at lower prices than roasted beans. But any savings disappears the moment you realize that you lose 10 percent weight if you roast light, more as you go darker. One failed roast batch wipes out any potential thrift, and every home-roast practitioner knows the inevitability of such failures.

That said, the thrill of the beans' aroma as they start to crackle, and those times when, after picking exactly the right moment to stop the roast, you see beans you brought to perfection…Ah. That's the moment you understand why few who take up home roasting can stop completely. It's hard not to get hooked. It has the long-lasting hobbyist appeal of a pastime that favors constant experiments. Some will be successful, but there may be more than a few undrinkable disasters. Plus, it's also fun.

After you have more information about home roasting, judge for yourself.

Getting Started with Home Roasting

If you want to roast at home, you need a good facility. Consider the following:

Space

Choose a space that allows you to spread out. Roasting requires fast action. When the beans are about to finish, you don't want to be looking around for your tools. Cleanup is also a factor. Beans shed their skins, called chaff, during roasting. Some beans have very little, some have a lot. Choose a space that you can easily sweep or vacuum.

PLAYING WITH FIRE: ROASTING GUIDE TO SAFETY

Although roasting is undeniably fun, keep in mind that beans roast at extremely high temperatures. Fires are a problem in the industry. Commercial roasting facilities, where machinery is at least as rugged as the best home units, still have roasting fires. Keep a fire extinguisher handy. If using a thermometer to measure internal bean temperature, know that it's difficult to measure these temperatures accurately. Always err on the side of common sense, especially with darker roasts because these beans can catch fire more easily.

< Roasting beans at home allows you total control of your coffee process, and there are few aromas as intoxicating as that of just-roasted beans.

Yield/Batch Size

Every coffee roaster produces the best coffee when you make its recommended batch capacity. In other words, follow directions about batch capability scrupulously. Don't exceed or halve. If you plan to sample various coffees, buy a small roaster such as those by Hearthware. They are easy, capable machines that smoke less than larger machines.

Smoke

All home roasting involves some smoke and aroma. Home roaster marketing literature compares roasting coffee to baking bread. That's not so. The early roasting stages smell less than wonderful and the later stages are smoky. Except for the Nesco, all roasters exhibit at least enough smoke to require ventilation near the roasting area.

Hearthware makes a vent you can pretty easily adapt and install in your home. Some home roasters position their roasting space to feed a bathroom vent or open a window and drape the vent outside. That could work, though it's not ideal. The garage is also an option. However, garages in many places get cold in the winter and warm/hot in the summer. Aside from the temperature affecting our own comfort—and how dedicated are you if you care about that?—it definitely affects roasting quality.

Weather

Even if you roast inside, you may notice that weather and climate affect your coffee. Like bakers, you will become attuned to the weather. And like your professional counterparts, you'll learn to adjust. Home roasting equipment is notoriously temperature-sensitive. An average coffee brewer will still heat water properly if the temperature drops. Not a home roasting machine. If the weather gets too cold, the roaster won't heat up properly. This means you may not be able to roast outdoors in January. Humidity also affects home roasters negatively, but more subtly. Your home roaster should still work if the humidity changes, but it's something to which you should pay attention.

Voltage

Did you know that your electric company's voltage fluctuates between 105 and 125 volts? If you're like me, you probably don't normally care. But now you have a reason to care. This fluctuation may mean little to most of your appliances, but to your home electric coffee roaster, it likely means the difference between hitting first crack and getting your roast right or ruining your roast and tossing it (likely into the compost heap).

END THE ROAST EARLY

Some roasting continues beyond the roasting process, for hours or even a day longer. Experience will teach you whether to end the roast slightly earlier to accommodate this effect. Paradoxically, some roasters actually seem to roast darker and then the beans lighten after roasting. How do you know what will happen? You'll only know by experience.

The Well-Equipped Home Roasting Kit

The following tools and implements should be part of any home roasting kit:

1 A home roaster to roast your beans. Your choices (among others) include a manual home roaster with a crank, an air popcorn popper, or a consumer electric drum or electric fluid air roaster. (See page 60 for an extensive tutorial about selecting a home roaster.)

2 Green whole bean coffee to roast

3 Roasting log to note time, temperature, and amount and type of beans used. Once you find a particular coffee's perfect flavor, you will want to replicate it.

4 A thermometer to measure the beans' temperature. Get a digital, instant-read thermometer (and if not instant, one that works quite fast) or one with a thin, flexible probe attached to a digital console. The tip of the thermometer needs to access the roasting beans' center. Note, inserting a thermometer is for the expert roaster only.

5 Digital kitchen scale to weigh your beans to ensure that you follow the amount recommended for your roaster

6 Dry measuring cup to use the amount specified in your electric model's instructions

7 Kitchen timer or clock to accurately track how long the beans have been roasting

8 A set of steel colanders for cooling the hot roasted beans

9 Storage containers with tight-fitting lids to keep the precious beans fresh. Mason jars work well.

A powerful heating element such as a stovetop (gas) or electric hot plate (not shown)

10 Heat-safe gloves (or protective oven mitts) to safely handle hot beans

A fire extinguisher (not shown) because roasting fires do happen

Choosing the Right Home Roaster

There are many home coffee roasters on the market, each with its own distinctive methods of heating beans. How much do you want to roast each time? How dark to you like your beans? In the remaining pages of this chapter, we explore the various models available and offer a practical guide to using each style.

Stovetop Roasting

In a stovetop roaster, coffee is roasted in an open or special closed pan placed on a gas stove burner. The person roasting the beans manually stirs with a crank handle to evenly distribute the beans during roasting. This method requires direct contact between a pan surface and the beans. Stovetop roasting takes advantage of something you already have a heat source. A variation of this method uses an oven pan with perforated holes.

Pros

- Long roast time. Like drum roasters, the stovetop roasters have a long roast cycle (likely the longest of all roasters), taking up to twenty minutes. This gives you a nice window and margin to stop the roast at just the right bean doneness.

- No noise. The only sounds come from the stove, the crank, and the crackling beans, which makes it easy to hear the nuanced first crack versus the faster second crack.

- Complex flavor. Longer roasts create coffee with more complexity. The stovetop roaster does this as well, if not better, than any other home method.

Cons

- Flame guesswork. At what level do you set the flame on the burner? It definitely takes trial and error. Keep track of how long it takes to roast a full cycle (anywhere from twelve to twenty minutes). Don't count cooling time, which is not part of the roast cycle.

- Crank speed. How fast do you turn the crank? The trick is to find a speed that allows the beans enough contact with the hot pan bottom but keeps all of the beans moving. You'll know to crank faster if you get scorched beans or if tipping occurs, in which the ends of beans turn black from too much hot surface contact.

- Inability to check beans' doneness. Stovetop roasters (or corn poppers doing double duty) require you to open the top to check on your beans, which also lets steam and heat escape. It's difficult to see the beans, even with the hatch open, so it takes trial and error to know when to stop roasting.

- Risk of flat taste. Just as stovetop roasters offer the opportunity to develop complexity, they also increase the risk of creating coffee that tastes flat. This happens after roasting beans at too low of a temperature for too long.

Materials

Thick metal enclosed coffee roasting pan with crank handle on top

Stovetop

Green coffee beans

Digital scale

Kitchen timer or clock

Roasting notebook

Heat-safe gloves

2 steel colanders

Mason jar (or other glass container)

Fire extinguisher, in case of roasting fire

< A stovetop roaster takes advantage of something you likely already have: a stove.

Stovetop Roasting (continued)

Expert Notes on Stovetop Roasting
Here are a few tips for stovetop roasting:

- Remove the chaff from the beans during cooling. Unfortunately, chaff can get messy. Consider cooling the beans outdoors or over a sink to contain the mess. (Chaff makes excellent compost.)

- Pull your roast into cooling just before the beans reach their desired doneness. This takes practice, but it's worth it to learn because coffee beans will continue to roast for at least a minute into the cooling stage.

- Break apart a roasted bean. If it is lighter inside than outside, try reducing roasting heat. If the interior is darker than the exterior, increase roasting heat.

- Roast beans for longer than ten minutes and less than twenty minutes to maximize your beans' potential flavor development and complexity and to prevent them from going flat.

Instructions

1. Place the cool roasting pan on the stovetop, centering it over the burner.

2. Weigh the green coffee beans using your digital scale based on the amount the manufacturer predetermined that the roaster can handle.

3. Open the hinged top hatch on the pan's top and pour the beans into the roaster **(a)**. Immediately turn the crank to evenly distribute the beans **(b)**.

4. Turn the burner to medium heat. Begin timer as you manually turn the crank slowly and constantly.

5. After 5 to 10 minutes, the beans will begin popping, indicating the start of the first crack stage. Note the time in your roasting notebook.

6. Listen closely to the beans. After a couple of minutes, all of the beans will have popped, followed by a brief silence. A minute or so later, a new, faster crackling sound, akin to logs on a fireplace, will start. It's often accompanied by hissing. At this point, open the hatch and look at the beans. Note their color and the time.

7. Use bean color to determine when they are done.

8. Don the heat-safe gloves. When your beans reach desired doneness, open the hatch and immediately pour them into one heat-safe colander **(c)**.

9. Pour the hot beans from one colander to the other until they are cool to touch (about 5 minutes). This process loosens the chaff, so it tends to float around. Blow the chaff away from the beans during tossing to remove as much of it as possible.

10. Once the beans cool enough to touch, transfer them into the mason jar (or other glass container). Leave the jar open and exposed to air for a few hours. Cap the jar before day's end. Do not leave the jar open overnight.

Stovetop Roasting Tutorial

Drum Roasting

In drum roasting, a perforated cylinder holds the beans, which get heated from below by radiant heat. The cylinder constantly rotates to evenly distribute heat across the beans. In addition, a steady stream of hot air blows through the cylinder's center, creating a heating environment much like a convection oven, encouraging a consistent, uniform roast. The majority of commercial operations use a drum method to roast their coffee.

Drum roasters are now available to home aficionados. Drum roasters run quietly and roast more slowly, which is designed to match the traditional flavor development of a commercial roaster in smaller home batches. The perforated cylinder on this Behmor drum roaster constantly rotates to evenly distribute heat across the beans (See photos on page 67).

Pros

- Long roast time. Drum roasters usually take between fifteen and twenty minutes to roast. This is good in general, but it can be stressful trying to hit the cooling cycle button at just that magic moment.

- Perfect yield. Drum roasters typically roast a half-pound of coffee, which many coffee drinkers consider just the right amount for their use. More generous hobbyists roast extras for friends—increasing their social standing considerably.

- Developed, complex flavor. Many in the coffee industry believe drum roasters offer great complexity of flavors. Whether this is due to longer roast times or type of heat compared to fluid-air roasting is the subject of intense debate. It calls for more taste tests.

- No noise. Most drum roasters are extremely quiet, allowing the roast master to listen for the subtle distinction of the first and second cracks.

Cons

- Bad visibility. Many drum roasters don't allow you to view the beans as they roast. This is a big disadvantage. Commercial drum roasters feature tryers, catchers that allows the roast master to remove bean samples to check their doneness. But most consumer drum machines don't have this feature, restricting you to listening and smelling.

- Slow cooling. Drum roasters typically dump the just-roasted beans onto a turntable. Commercial machines feature forced air to speed cooling, but most home machines don't. Rapid cooling ensures that your beans stop roasting when you choose to stop roasting them. Most experts believe rapid cooling improves flavor.

Materials

Green beans

Digital scale

Drum roaster

Heat-safe gloves

Mason jar (or other glass container)

Fire extinguisher, in case of roasting fire

Drum Roasting (continued)

Expert Notes on Drum Roasting

Here are some tips on drum roasting:

- If your home drum roaster does not offer in-cylinder cooling, use oven mitts or heat-safe gloves to carefully pour roasted beans into colander following the roast. Then pour them into a second colander. Repeat this back-and-forth process to cool the beans. Some advanced home roasters prefer this method to in-machine cooling, claiming it is faster and therefore better at halting the roasting process.

- If the roaster offers pre-timed cycles, choose one that will likely roast darker (longer) than you wish. You can always stop a cycle in the middle.

- True believers in home roasting can go as far as modifying a gas barbeque grill to roast up to three pounds (1.4 kg) of beans per load. One roaster even gutted his backyard grill and paid a local sheet metal worker to fashion a proprietary perforated metal drum designed to spin using a rotisserie attachment. His grill roaster has been so successful that he's become a weekly attraction at his local farmers' markets.

Instructions

1. Measure the recommended amount of green beans using your digital scale and pour them into open end of the cylinder.

2. Gently shake cylinder to evenly distribute the beans **(a)**.

3. Seat the cylinder (drum) into the machine's track to ensure it turns properly. Add the chaff collector **(b)**.

4. Start the drum roaster. Always begin with a cool machine unless otherwise directed by the manufacturer.

5. Wait for the popping sound to begin, indicating the first crack stage.

6. Once the beans finish popping, a brief silence will occur before the beans begin their second crack, a faster sound reminiscent of crackling fireplace logs. Begin the cooling cycle at any time from this point.

7. Don your heat-safe gloves. After the cooling cycle ends, open and empty the chaff collector **(c)**.

8. Carefully remove the drum from the machine **(d)** and pour the beans into a glass jar for storage.

9. Following each roast, blow any remaining chaff out of the machine.

Drum Roasting Tutorial

Fluid-Air Roasting

In this method, developed in the mid-1900s, beans roast by floating on a bed of hot air. Its commercial predecessor was the Jabez-Burns Thermalo drum roaster noteworthy for using a stream of heated fluid air shot through the drum's center, producing similar results. In the fluid-air roasting method, hot air lifts the unroasted beans until they float; the suspension of the beans ensures even roasting. The process is similar to that of an electric popcorn popper, and in fact, can work using a popcorn popper. The noise of the circulating air often masks the crucial popping sounds, but the ability to see the beans during roasting means you more likely know when they are done.

Look for the airborne beans on the left, lifted high by the hot air shooting upwards from below.

Pros

- Ease. Fluid-air roasting is most efficient roast method because it roasts in a linear method and thus is the easiest for which to design a machine. Best of all, home air roasting requires no fancy gear. A simple air popcorn popper will do.

- Roasting speed. Air roasting is fast and heats beans evenly, bringing out the coffee's bright acidity and reducing any tipping (or scorching of the beans) that frequently happens in drum roasts. Air roasting generally takes between five and twelve minutes.

- Visual presentation. Most fluid-air roasters use glass canisters for roasting. Not only does the roast master get the pleasure of seeing the beans roast but also can use this tool to watch the beans and judge their doneness.

- Quick cooling. Most air roasters feature quick-responding cooling cycles. Many experts believe that quick cooling reduces bitterness.

Cons

- Speed. The air roaster's quick roasting speed may improve flavor, but it means a quick response when the beans finish roasting. Seconds count, and an early or late response at the moment of truth can ruin the batch.

- Too much noise. It takes significant air movement to keep a bed of beans floating, and that means noise, often enough to make it difficult to hear first and second crack.

- Low yield. Most air roasters can roast only a small amount of beans, perhaps enough for a pot or two of coffee.

- No flavor complexity. Some claim that air roasting, while simple and straightforward, does not develop the same complexity and flavor depth of a good drum roast. Most who share this view think it has something to do with air's convection heating, although some direct contact heat does occur as the beans touch each other.

Materials

Fluid-air coffee roaster

Digital scale

Green coffee beans

Kitchen timer or clock

Heat-safe gloves

Steel colander, optional

Mason jar (or other glass container)

Fire extinguisher, in case of roasting fire

Fluid-Air Roasting (continued)

Overriding the System

Many advanced users prefer to decide exactly when to stop the roast rather than let the preprogrammed appliance do it for them. To override the preset cycles, choose the longest roast cycle, perhaps longer than you expect. Once the beans achieve their desired roast, simply hit cool to manually end the process.

Instructions

1. Start with a cool roaster, unless otherwise specified by the manufacturer.

2. Using your digital scale, measure the manufacturer's recommended amount of green beans for the roaster's capacity **(a)**. Do not exceed the recommended volume.

3. Pour the beans into the roaster **(b)**. Gently shake to spread them evenly. Press start. Start your timer here as well.

4. Observe the beans as they turn yellow **(c)**.

5. As soon as a crackling sound begins, the coffee has reached the leading edge of first crack. Note the time. All beans should be at first crack within 1 to 2 minutes **(d)**. Once all the beans have reached first crack, a brief silence will occur, followed by second crack, distinguished by a more rapid crackling sound. The beginning of second crack delivers a Full City roast **(e)**. Beyond this temperature darker roasts such Vienna and French occur.

6. When your beans have reached their desired doneness, press the cooling button to override the roaster's heating (or allow your roaster to automatically cool when the timer ends). Your roaster will switch to its cooling cycle and begin circulating fresh, cool air. (If using a corn popper that doesn't have a cooling cycle, wear oven mitts and carefully remove the roaster's canister and pour the hot beans into a heat-safe colander.)

7. When the cooling cycle ends, the roaster will turn itself off. Immediately remove the beans from the machine and allow them to cool for at least 1 hour before packaging for storage.

8. Once they cool completely, transfer to a mason jar or another airtight container.

9. Clean the chaff from all roaster parts after each use **(f)**.

Fluid-Air Roasting Tutorial

Using a Thermometer with Your Home Roaster

The directions above were purposely written minus any temperature guidelines. The internal bean temperature is probably the best and most useful data for roasting, and yet it is the most difficult information to reliably obtain (even for commercial roasters). Installing a thermometer will ensure that you can get some temperature reading during roasting.

It is impossible to actually stick a thermometer inside a coffee bean to know its exact temperature. The best we can do is approximate by measuring the air temperature directly next to a bean or group of beans. Note, the temperature reading is almost always close to but not exactly the beans' actual temperature. Heat from the roasting machine itself and other factors will interfere with a true reading. With this caveat in mind, it is still useful to install a thermometer. The goal is to find a fast-reacting one; you want to know the temperature now, not what it was a minute ago.

The best place to insert the thermometer probe is within a cluster of beans, away from direct roaster heat. Using a thermometer in drum roasters is difficult because you need to keep the probe in the beans, yet away from moving parts. However, the most challenging roaster design from which to get an accurate reading is an air roaster because of the need to find a location away from moving air, where beans cluster.

It is tricky to do this with just two hands, but it is possible to lift the hatch on a stovetop roaster and insert a thermometer to check bean doneness. This needs to happen quickly so the beans won't scorch while the crank stands idle.

Make the Machine Work for You

Some rogue home roasters will modify their machines by drilling holes into the body so their thermometers can access the beans from an ideal location. Naturally, this invasive method voids all machine warranties, so do this only if you accept full responsibility for damage. You also can purchase a thermometer with a flexible, narrow probe that will wind around and into your roaster—with no physical modification necessary.

Quick Home-Roasting Temperature Guide

Determining when your home-roasted beans are done requires a combination of sensory cues from the visual, aural, and aromatic. Refer to this quick guide when monitoring your roasting batches.

ROAST STYLE	BEAN TEMPERATURE	APPEARANCE	SMELL	SOUND
Cinnamon/ New England (Light)	420°F (216°C)	Light brown	No roast smoke. Bright baking-cookies aroma	First crack popping, silence, then initial second crack (crackling fireplace) sound
City/Full City	430°F (221°C)	Medium brown	Slight light smoke. Baking-bread aroma	First crack popping, silence, then initial second crack (crackling fireplace) sound
Vienna	440°F (227°C)	Dark brown with very light spots	Smoke. Slight burned aroma	First, second crack are equal parts
French	445°F (229°C)	Dark brown with oil spots	Thick smoke that annoys the spouse or roommate	First crack, then second crack for longer
Espresso	448°F (231°C)	Darker brown with full oil coat	Very smoky (think bar smoke)	First crack, then second crack even longer than for French roast

PART TWO

THE BREW

4 GRINDING

GRINDING beans and brewing coffee are arguably the most important parts to the art and craft of coffee. No matter how great the coffee beans, how carefully they've been cared for, or the skill with which they were processed, packaged, shipped, and roasted, they don't become "coffee" until ground and brewed. The good news? If you can fill a coffee scoop, press a button, and use a kitchen scale, you can make great coffee.

By the end of this chapter, you will know how to do the following:

• Differentiate grinder types

• Select the grinder that's appropriate for you

• Grind coffee properly

< Manual grinders aren't just for antique buyers.

Grinders and Grinding

Since you presumably start with beans rather than already-ground coffee, we'll cover grinding before brewing. If you use preground beans, skip to chapter 5, "Brewing," which starts on page 89.

Why can't you just put coffee beans into a filter, run hot water over them, and brew coffee? Theoretically you can. The question is, when does it become the finished, brewed beverage known as coffee? If you simply soak beans in hot water, eventually the water turns brown. By the time it becomes dark, rich coffee, it will be cold. Someone discovered many years ago that mashing the beans into smaller pieces (what we call grinding) speeds up the brewing process.

The Turks, who pushed millstones around to grind grain, get credit for inventing the coffee grinder. They used one corrugated plate and one flat plate. One was stationary; the other moved. This system created almost powder-like, very fine grinds. Coarser grinds became popular with more modern brewing methods, as inventors realized the flavor connection between grinding beans to a certain size and the finished coffee's taste. Other coffee-drinking countries adapted grinds to fit their brewing methods. Today, grinding's role is straightforward. The finer ground the beans, the more intense flavor they produce and the less time it takes to extract that flavor. This is because with finer ground coffee, hot water touches more surface area during brewing.

A coffee grinder's only job is to granulize coffee beans into exact and (theoretically) same-sized particles. Some coffee lovers mistakenly think that a range of particle sizes, like a mix of light and dark roasted beans, offers a variety of tastes. Not true! Each brewing method has its own perfect particle size based on how long the particles will touch the grounds. The longer the brew time is, the larger the particles should be. Smaller-than-ideal particles add bitterness due to overextraction. Larger-than-ideal particles underextract, causing weak flavor and waste.

Invest in a good grinder to enjoy the best coffee possible. Get in the habit of grinding just before you brew. This will result in a more pungent aroma and fresher tasting coffee. Plus, some of the best available roasted coffees will open up to you, as some of the characters who roast these precious beans won't even consider grinding them before shipping. If you home roast, preground coffee is obviously not a consideration.

Here are average coffee ground particles shown to scale:

1 Pulverized average particle size: 100 microns

2 Espresso average particle size: 200 microns

3 Fine/vacuum average particle size: 500 microns

4 Drip average particle size: 600 microns

5 Automatic drip average particle size: 800 microns in the United States and 580 microns in Europe

6 Coarse grind average particle size: 1,000 microns

The Case for Grinding at Home

Industrial rollers produce the most consistent grind possible, making industrial grinding, by far, the best method. It exceeds even the best home machine's ability to control one of the most important variables: particle size. So why do I recommend grinding at home? It's freshness. Freshness is an important reason for most coffee lovers because it's critical for enjoying the kind of coffee aroma and flavor we all want.

Life is a series of tradeoffs; there is just too much coffee character lost in coffee ground after roasting, rather than before brewing. This is not a subtle difference.

Most preground coffees don't stay fresh for long. Preground canned coffees are purposefully exposed to air after grinding, which removes much of their freshness. This process, called degassing, is done to prevent cans from buckling during their product life.

Beans and preground coffees treated with nitrogen flushing as they are packaged into one-way valve bags stay fresh for about ninety days, much longer than the two weeks of freshness of beans sold in simple fold-over unsealed sacks. One-way bags feature a ringlike indentation with a hole in the center and are clearly visible. Why does this coffee stay longer? Nitrogen flushing minimizes contact with oxygen and protects coffee from elements that hasten staling. However, by design, one-way valves allow carbon dioxide to escape. As the carbon dioxide goes, so do the smells and aromas your taste buds identify with freshness. To date, no coffee packaging method preserves aroma and flavor or allows the coffee to improve over time, as with some wines.

BEWARE OF FRESHNESS DATES

Packaging companies create freshness dates to try to please large coffee companies, which understandably want to build in time to transport and warehouse their products. At best, freshness dates reliably prevent rancidity, but they rarely predict freshness. Seek out packages with actual roast dates (rather than freshness dates) and try to use the product immediately or freeze it within ninety days of the date.

Properly packaged and dated preground coffee also has a ninety-day freshness window, but then goes stale quickly after the package's seal is broken. Freezing after opening adds additional product life. See the section "Freezing Coffee Beans" on page 43 in chapter 2 for extensive information about freezing green and roasted beans.

Look for a roasting date rather than a freshness date to determine coffee's freshness.

Grinding For The Roast

Does roast darkness affect grind? The short answer is yes. Darker roasts need to be ground slightly coarser. A coffee bean's brittleness increases the longer and darker it roasts and the more moisture driven from it. The increased brittleness causes it to fracture into smaller particles than a lighter roast. This increases the coffee's bitterness and strength. Consider setting your grinder a notch coarser for dark roasted beans.

Choosing a Grinder

The best grinder is one that consistently produces even-sized particles. Though it seems obvious, determining which grinder does this is not so simple.

Tests called ro-tap tests determine a grinder's grind consistency. A ro-tap test involves placing a grinder's resulting grounds atop a series of sieves with different-sized holes and measuring the range and percentages that seep through. One place to look for these test results is my website, www.coffeecompanion.com.

Look for mathematical grounds-distribution results from these screen tests. You want the grinder that produces the biggest percentage of identical grounds the ideal size for your brewer. In the section, "Determining the Right Grind for Your Brewer" on page 85, I've published the recommended numbers in microns for each grind. Note, the larger the holes in the test screen or sieve, the smaller its screen-size number. For instance, a size twenty sieve has larger screen holes than a size forty sieve.

Blade Grinders

Most inexpensive grinders have spinning blades, hence the name blade grinder. These are notoriously bad for grinding coffee.

FINES: COFFEE GRINDING BAD GUYS

The word "fines" describes 200 to 300 micron-size waste particles produced during grinding. Although all grind specifications allow—and even benefit from—a certain percentage of small fines, any amount beyond 30 percent harms the coffee's flavor. There are also tinier 100 to 200 micron superfines, which clog filters and add bitterness in virtually any amount to almost any brew. Calling them bitters might be more accurate. You can't do anything to alter the amount of fines your grinder produces, but you can seek out a grinder with an industry-accepted amount. If you notice coffee clumps in your container of just-ground coffee, exclude these from your brewer.

To use it, pour a premeasured amount of beans into the top, which contains the spinning propeller. As you push a power button, the blades begin to spin, cutting through the beans. The blade's whirling motion helps create an air vacuum that draws the beans into the propeller's path.

In practice, this random method often requires shaking the grinder to get any semblance of equal grinding. Even as the grounds get finer and appear more consistent, microscopic examination or a screen test will reveal a wide variance. Also, using a blade grinder causes its tiny motor, located just under the curved metal plate, to heat up the grounds. Many of these grinders come with warnings not to run the motor for more than one minute or risk heat affecting your grounds enough to actually release some taste and aroma.

If you're not already sold on not using one of these grinders, consider this: They are unpredictable in terms of how fine they grind. One time, it may produce coffee fine for a drip coffee maker. Another time, it may be too coarse or too fine. For espresso, the exact 200 to 250 micron grind particle size for the thirty-second extraction is so critical that you really can't consider using a blade grinder.

Burr Grinders

Burr grinders, sometimes called disc or mill grinders, are the kind to use. You set the grinder's range, which then limits size by the distance between the two grinding pieces. Set the gap between the two discs or cones by click stops (stops on your grinder) so you can simply dial your required fineness and assure batch-to-batch consistency.

How does a burr grinder work? A rotating flat metal disc or conical cone fits inside a second, stationary disc or cone. As a chute between the two grinding pieces feeds the beans, flutes that become progressively finer cut them. The coarse surface on one of the discs then grinds them. This design grinds the beans much more consistently than a blade.

Still, burrs are not perfect. They require careful alignment. They wear down through use and as they do, the grind may drift and become less consistent. Also, some modern marketing touts features such as their timers or the ability of parts of the container to go in the dishwasher. Instead, look for hardened steel discs (what the best grinders use).

Each of the two types of burr grinders—conical and flat—has inherent advantages. Typically, conical burrs work better for coarse grinding, whereas disc burrs are preferred for finer grinding.

Inexpensive blade grinders don't grind coffee well.

Choose a burr grinder if you can. They are available in several styles. A Jericho grinder is shown here with its exposed burr.

Instructions

To use a burr grinder, follow these steps:

1. Measure the desired coffee amount and weigh the beans **(a)**.

2. Place the beans in the grinder hopper, which is usually located at top **(b)**.

3. Turn the grinder on. Most electric coffee grinders are loud. Even with quieter models, you can usually tell when the beans are ground. To be sure, check the hopper for stuck beans.

4. Once the grounds sound finished, remove thereceptacle that holds them. Check for ground fines clumping. If possible, remove any clumps and discard. (It makes great compost!).

5. Fill your filter with finished grounds **(c)**.

Generally speaking, a burr grinder will serve you best. Some claim that fast grinders produce more fines and superfines, but my less-than-scientific tests of various grinders do not demonstrate any correlation. My own prized hand grinder did most poorly in our tests and my super fast Ditting electric grinder did better than any consumer machine. Of course, the Ditting is more than 1,000 dollars, so the build quality should be first rate.

Coated burrs last longer and maintain grind calibration. Expect to pay anywhere from 50 to 1,100 dollars for a good grinder. Cost is not the lone deciding factor. If you're really a player, investigate restaurant suppliers. Some of these grinders are large, however, so keep the SAF (Spouse Acceptance Factor) in mind. Someday someone will invent something like a laser cut home coffee grinder that simply does the quantum physics necessary to give you exact, evenly cut pieces from your beans. Until then, seek out the best grinder you can find to grind fresh and consistently even coffee.

Burr Grinder Tutorial

Manual Grinders

You may have seen hand-powered manual burr grinders, particularly in antique shops. Zassenhaus in Germany still makes a fairly well-known model. These units are attractive, probably sold more often as conversation pieces and decorative items than working grinders. But don't dismiss them. The dedicated coffee enthusiast may use a hand-powered wooden grinder while traveling. Why give up fresh ground coffee on vacation? Know that bean hoppers are small, which may mean filling and grinding twice for a decent-size batch. But the grind mechanism in the Zassenhaus is a true conical-disc burr grinder, as is the case for most antique models. Some match the best electric grinders in overall grind quality.

Wall- or table-mounted hand grinders are also options. Some of them do an excellent job grinding. No electric grinder really uses all that much power, but it's a nice feeling knowing you're not using any. Some people even consider it a mild workout.

Though probably sold more as decorative items than working grinders, some manual grinders match the best electric grinders in overall grind quality.

ATTENTION COLLECTORS

Large wagon wheel grinders fetch big money at auctions and at collectors' shows. If you spot one, you'll instantly recognize it. These are unusually easy to use because of the large wheel (some are actually too large to fit in the average kitchen). They also do a great job of grinding coffee.

Grinder Maintenance

Grinders require little in the way of maintenance, but there are a few checks you should make regularly, including the following:

- Check your grinder's exposed parts from time to time for grinds accumulation. Use a brush—an old toothbrush will do—to remove grounds. A dry brush tends to work more effectively than a damp or wet one.

- Wash removable, dishwasher-safe hoppers in the top rack once per month to remove any oil buildup. If you frequently grind dark roast coffees, you may wish to increase this washing to once a week.

- Wash the receptacle between each use. A sponge and some soapy water will do the trick. Avoid scented dishwasher detergents.

- Use oats to remove flavor oils from a grinder that has ground flavored coffee. These flavor oils stick to your grinder's mechanism and will likely change your non-flavored beans' taste. Once my wife was entertaining her aunts, and one of them brought as a housewarming gift some flavored coffee, which they ran through the grinder. Horrified, I spent a sleepless night considering how to save one of my favorite coffee grinders. Oats worked perfectly. They are soft enough to run through the grinder, gentle on the burrs, and absorb the flavor oils. However, let me emphatically state that you should not regularly grind flavored coffee in a grinder dedicated to non-flavored coffee.

- Avoid using your coffee grinder as a spice mill, unless you have a separate unit for this purpose. Blade grinders are supposedly terrific for this use. You should still purchase a separate grinder because ground coffee is a flavor and aroma sponge.

Determining the Right Grind for Your Brewer

In addition to selecting the right grinder, you need to select the right grind. The following are basic guidelines for various grinds, moving from finest to coarsest:

Warning: Most novices grind too fine. Start out grinding coarser than you think you'll need. Then move a notch at a time finer until you reach the perfect grind and taste.

Pulverized Grind

With this grind, coffee is as fine as flour. If you dip your fingers into Turkish ground coffee, which is typically pulverized, your fingers should come out coated with dust. Blade grinders could likely produce this grind, but you would lose aroma and flavor due to overheating. Consumer burr grinders rarely have the calibration to grind this fine.

A friend who's an archaeology professor uses a mortar and pestle, which seems to work extraordinarily well. It can crush the beans to the required fineness without heating them up. For Turkish coffee devotees, get a mortar and pestle, which is easy to use and maintain and costs far less than the other less-likely-to-be-successful alternatives. Average particle size is 100 microns.

Espresso Grind

We devote an entire chapter of this book to Espresso, so we'll only touch on it here to present it as a grinding option and so you can see where in the fine-coarse continuum it falls. For more information about espresso, see chapter 6, "Espresso," which begins on page 127. Average particle size is 200 microns.

Fine/Vacuum Grind

This fine grind should almost, but not quite, be a powder. If you stick your finger in and pull it out, most of the coffee should not cling. It is designed for vacuum coffee brewers (discussed in chapter 5, "Brewing," page 89) that typically feature three-minute extraction times. It also is appropriate for manual one-cup Melitta-style V-shaped cone filters or half batches of larger brewers that feature a three- to four-minute contact time (also see chapter 5). Average particle size is 500 microns.

Drip Grind

Most modern canned coffees use this grind, which is coarser than vacuum. It contains no powder and is designed for four- to six-minute contact times. It is coarser than table salt, but it should feature table salt's pouring ability. The grounds should not cling together. Any brewing method that uses gravity—such as with drip coffee—needs grounds coarse enough to allow the water to pass easily through under its own weight. Average particle size is 500 microns and larger.

Automatic Drip Grind

These grounds start to resemble kosher salt. Designed for use in metal filter baskets typically found in electric percolators, this grind stands up to six- to eight-minute contact time. Therefore, it can work for any brewer that takes longer than six minutes to brew or any method in which a metal filter containing holes allows small particles through and into your cup, such as a press pot (most often used with a three- to four-minute contact time, regardless of grind) or flip drip maker (see chapter 5, "Brewing").

If your automatic drip maker uses an underpowered electric heating element and chugs away brewing coffee for ten or twelve minutes, use coarse grounds. This helps the ground coffee endure the "long hot summer" of prolonged contact time. Bunn's flat-bottomed automatic drip uses an uncommonly brief three-minute contact time, yet its makers recommend a slightly coarser grind, claiming the brewer uses turbidation (mild water pressure from the spray head) to agitate the grounds and thus achieve more efficient extraction. Of course, your taste buds must micro-manage the final determinant in your machine's grind fineness setting. Average particle size is 800 microns (American auto drip). Europeans favor a smaller grind size averaging 580 microns.

Coarse Grind

This grind is a catchall for any method that takes longer than eight minutes and/or features filters likely to leak tiny grind particles into the final batch. Giant commercial coffee brewers that steep coffee in cloth sacks called urns use coarse grinds, as do such novelty brews as cowboy or campfire coffee, where grounds are tossed into an open vessel with boiling water (see chapter 5, "Brewing"). Average particle size is 1,000 microns.

In 1948, a voluntary group of coffee roasting companies agreed on these standards, which the United States Department of Commerce then published.

The specs haven't changed a bit since 1948, and they are credible. Unlike almost every other area of coffee, the industry found consensus and objective by-the-numbers proof about grinding. Would you buy a car without knowing its mileage first? Hopefully, further research into getting the best grinder will cause people to start asking the right questions. Instead of useless circuitry-like timers, coffee grinder manufacturers will begin publishing specifications that indicate how closely their products meet these specs.

So is grind important? Yes. For a great coffee, you need the right grind. The wrong one can actually change a coffee's taste.

GET TO KNOW YOUR AUTO DRIP

To figure out how fine to grind beans for your auto drip maker, time it. If it takes less than three minutes to brew, grind finer. If it takes more than six minutes, grind coarser. Finer grinding slows the coffee's gravitational pull down through the grounds, which further increases contact time with hot water and speeds the flavor release.

Any change in grind particle size will affect drip coffee's strength, making it the most dependent of any brewing method on the correct grind. Grinding too fine exposes more surface area and slows down drip rate, making your coffee stronger. Conversely, grinding too coarse exposes less surface area and speeds up drip rate, resulting in weaker coffee.

5 BREWING

NOW that we've got ground coffee, the real fun begins. Learning how to brew properly can immeasurably improve your coffee's quality. Even the most refined, seasoned experts acknowledge that a properly brewed cup of mediocre coffee tastes better than an improperly brewed cup made from the best beans.

All brewing methods must accomplish the following:

- Expose hot water to direct contact with ground coffee for an exact time period, enough to extract the flavor but not the bitterness

- Extract a percentage of flavors from a given formula. (Most consumers want 18 to 22 percent extraction by weight. Use the formula of two tablespoons [10 g] coffee beans per six ounces [180 ml] of water.)

- Control the water temperature at 200°F (93°C), hot enough to extract the full flavors but not so hot that it overextracts bitterness

- Remove or filter the grounds from the finished brew

Each coffee brewing method discussed in this chapter accomplishes these tasks. The rules may seem simple, but brewing is not an exact science because the variables constantly change. If you don't think you're doing it right, don't worry. Most of us don't do it right initially. An automatic brewer usually doesn't do it right either.

There is no process with more possibilities and variables than brewing. Every method allows for seemingly endless tweaks. A few moments spent analyzing your first brew will often offer some instructive changes for the next one. Once you finesse a taste formula, use it until you finish that batch of beans.

By the end of this chapter, you will know the basic brewing parameters and how to do the following:

- Fine tune your brewing formula for different varieties and roasts

- Brew coffee as well as any expert

< Brewing: The coffee lover's most important stage.

The Well-Equipped Brewing Kit

In addition to your brewer and grinder, the following tools and implements compose any good brewing kit. (A more extensive tutorial about selecting a brewer follows on pages 95–125.)

1 A digital or instant-read thermometer (or if not instant, one that works quite fast) or one with a thin, flexible probe attached to a digital console. For accurate, useful temperature readings, the tip of the thermometer needs to access the spot where the grounds and water mix.

2 A digital kitchen scale to weigh your beans ensures that you will keep your brew formula consistent and allows you to more easily make micro-adjustments. Choose a scale that measures to the ounce or gram; most people brew coffee from relatively small grounds quantities.

3 A timing device like a kitchen timer or clock accurately tracks how long the hot water and coffee grounds have been in contact and ensures consistency in brewing formulas.

4 A coffee scoop. Often one comes with your brewer. If not, food or specialty stores carry them. A coffee scoop ensures accurate, consistent measurements.

5 A tea kettle to make it easier to pour scalding water for manual brew methods such as French press. However, a saucepan (or microwave-safe vessel) will also do.

A powerful heating element such as a stovetop (electric or gas) or electric hot plate either to heat water for pouring or to heat the brewer itself (not shown)

6 Heat-safe gloves or protective oven mitts for safely handling hot coffee brewers and tea kettles

Water (not shown). Bottled spring water is the best quality, but tap is fine if your local water has suitable qualities. (For more about water, see page 92)

7 A liquid measuring cup to ensure consistent water amounts

8 Fresh whole bean coffee, the freshest available. Grind only before brewing. (For more about selecting coffee, see chapter 2.)

9 Storage containers with tight-fitting lids to keep the precious beans as fresh as possible. (For more on storage, see chapter 2.)

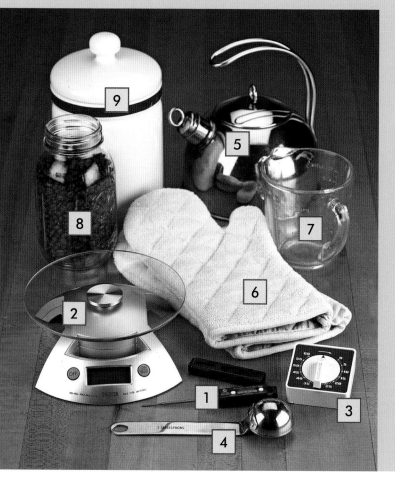

Brewing Temperature and Contact Time

In all brewing methods, exposing ground coffee to water extracts the coffee's flavor. Theoretically, you could soak roasted coffee beans in a pitcher of water and eventually the water would become coffee. But certain temperatures and time facilitate extraction of oils contained in coffee beans more quickly and in an aromatic and flavorful manner.

The recipe for making excellent coffee is well-established: Two tablespoons (10 g) per six ounces (180 ml) of water. It has been documented that Ludwig von Beethoven used to count sixty beans for each six-ounce (180 ml) cup—which happens to equal two tablespoons (10 g). Unless noted otherwise, this formula applies to all brewing methods.

This formula is an important starting point, but slight adjustments may produce a better batch, one that tastes better *to you.* Treat this formula as a relatively foolproof guide—*guide* being the operative word. Different coffee roasts, different origin coffees, and brewing-temperature variations affect strength and flavor. For instance, to brew a forty-eight ounce

(1,440 ml) batch (eight six-ounce [180 ml] cups), begin with sixteen tablespoons (80 g) of whole beans. If the coffee turns out too strong, pull back to fourteen tablespoons (70 g); if it's too weak, increase the beans to eighteen tablespoons (90 g). (And here's a tip: Always treat your first batch of a new coffee as a test batch.)

Temperature

Although any temperature water will eventually become coffee if in contact with beans for long enough, hot water is the fastest means to this end. (It also results in a hot beverage which, historically, is the way most people prefer to drink coffee.) Water heated to 200°F (93°C) plus or minus a few degrees is considered the standard benchmark. Water not heated as high is less efficient. Water heated higher extracts bitter flavors.

Time

The longer the coffee grounds are exposed to water, the more the flavor is extracted. The shorter the grounds are exposed, the less the flavor is extracted. The appropriate average time varies by grind; a drip grind takes four to six minutes, but a coarse grind can take up to eight minutes. If using a manual machine that steeps the coffee in a reservoir, such as a vacuum or press pot, you can easily vary the contact time between the grounds and water. Press pot coffee with a finer grind and longer extraction time will taste significantly different than one with a coarser grind and shorter extraction time. (See chapter 4, "Grinding," for more information.)

TAKE ITS TEMPERATURE

How do you know whether your automatic brewer is performing to spec? Simple: Take its temperature. Hold a fast-acting thermometer in the stream of brewing coffee as the water emerges from the basket of grounds. The temperature should be more or less at the 200°F (93°C) mark.

Water

The chemical makeup of the strongest cup of coffee is roughly 1.35 percent dissolved coffee solids. The rest, approximately 98.65 percent, is water. Water plays two roles in coffee. It complements the taste and acts as the solvent that seduces the coffee essence from the grounds.

Let's address water's taste first. Water's flavor varies quite a bit around the world. Assuming it is potable, or healthy to drink, its chemical makeup can include different amounts of several ingredients. Calcium, which comes from rocks in the ground, is the largest likely suspect. Have you heard the phrase "hard water"? It usually refers to the calcium minerals within it. If the minerals in hard water are in high enough concentration, they can give the coffee a pronounced metallic taste.

Some say hard water extracts coffee poorly during brewing. Actually, this is less than true, although hard water does present problems. During brewing, the near-boiling water keeps calcium and other minerals suspended. Some cling to the pipes inside of the coffee brewer, clogging it after awhile. At least the minerals don't affect actual brewing ability.

Water softened using salt—found in most homes and some municipalities—is more problematic. The residual salt following softening can form a gelatin-like goo in the coffee brewer's filter, which can prevent extraction or even halt the whole process.

pH Level

Liquid's acid-versus-alkaline value, represented by pH, can significantly affect coffee's taste. Water should be 7.1, a neutral pH, for its role in coffee flavor. Acidic or alkaline water will throw off the finished beverage's flavor balance. Alkaline water in particular, when used to brew dark roasts, can cause a dull, indistinct taste.

Water Checklist

Water for brewing should be as follows:

- One hundred total dissolved solids (tds) or less. This is soft- to medium-hard water. It will taste better and extend the useful product life of your brewing equipment without the need to delime (remove the mineral buildup).

- A pH level of 7.1. Water more acidic can accentuate coffee bean taste defects. Water more alkaline can make coffee taste bland. That said, if you can only brew using alkaline water, think light roasts. If your water is more acidic, consider darker roasts.

- Chlorine-free water. If you can smell or taste any chlorine in water you use to brew, expect the chlorine to affect your coffee's taste. Get rid of the chlorine by using a charcoal filter or letting the coffee sit for an hour or so until the chlorine evaporates.

Does this mean you must use bottled water? In many cases, municipal (tap) water will brew excellent coffee. Most municipalities post their water specifications on their websites. Most likely, the water will contain chlorine, as many places overchlorinate to prevent contamination. As we mention above, chlorine is easy to address. Excess minerals and less-than-ideal pH levels, while less common, are harder to fix. If you come across this, consider using bottled water. Keep in mind that all bottled waters are not alike. Just as with tap water, verify the pH level and tds of bottled water before using.

Filters

By design, coffee filters separate grounds from brewed coffee following brewing. All coffee brewing processes involve some sort of filtration. Even the earliest (and simplest) brewing methods—tossing loose grounds into a pot of boiling water—used "filtration" by carefully pouring off the coffee, keeping the grounds separate from the finished beverage.

Filters differ in their ability to remove all grounds and sediment from the brewed coffee. This influences the perception of coffee's taste, body, and texture. Some people prefer a super-clean, highly filtered beverage; others prefer one rich in sediment. Filtration methods that allow particles to pass through to the finished brew will affect taste (and bitterness). The tiniest particles continue to extract in the finished beverage.

Your personal taste—and your brewer's function, of course—affect which filter you choose. Any time you change filter types, figure out contact time to make sure the new filter does not require finer or coarser grinds. A thicker paper will prolong contact; a fine metal mesh one will accelerate it. (The irony of this is that manufacturers often tout the "full body and rich flavor" metal filters produce, but speeding up the drip rate actually reduces contact time and weakens coffee strength.)

Clockwise from top:

1 Metal mesh filter

2 Percolater metal filter

3 Espresso porta-filter

4 Paper filters, both bleached and natural

Filters (continued)

Most metal mesh filters included with drip makers prevent a significant amount of particles in the finished brew, although they tend to increase flow rates and thus reduce water's contact time with the grounds.

Glass filters, used in some older vacuum brewer models, contain tiny surface bumps that create a sieve in the upper bowl's glass tube, allowing liquid but not grinds to pass through. Most glass filters create an excellent pot of coffee, but they break easily.

Some antique vacuum coffee makers use cloth filters, which, in general, do an excellent filtering job. Also, modern, reusable cloths are an ecologically savvy choice. However, they are difficult to find and keep clean. Cloth tends to accumulate grounds and oils. When using cloth filters, discard if mold appears.

Some coffee buffs accuse paper filters of not letting all of the coffee's flavors through. More accurately, paper holds back sediment and thus results in an ultra-clean brew. Some paper filters now intentionally have holes that resemble mesh filters' holes, allowing comparable sediment amounts to pass. Paper does not prevent the passage of oils, the most important flavor component.

Some people claim that bleached paper filters gives the brew a bitter chlorine taste. Though most paper filters are bleached with hydrogen peroxide, this is flavorless and odorless. (When in doubt, rinse a paper filter in cold water before using it to remove any possible taste.) Unbleached paper filters *do* have a distinct taste and odor, which is difficult to avoid. For all-around flavor, use hydrogen peroxide bleached paper filters.

Each paper filter ends up in the trash after use, which raises some concern about their environmental impact. Weigh this against the impact of cleaning and caring for permanent filters. Paper filters break down in compost along with coffee grounds.

Illustrated Brewing Techniques

This section offers step-by-step instructions for several of the world's most popular brewing methods, each of which has been thoroughly tested by coffee aficionados and should be a great starting point for the coffee newbie. Once you master the basics, feel free to improvise on your own.

A classic automatic drip brewer in action.

Manual Drip

To make manual drip coffee, tiny droplets of water flow over the coffee grounds and allow the coffee to drip through, extracting oils from the grounds as they pass. Gravity and the amount of grounds control the contact time between grounds and water. More grounds take more time through which to pass, increasing the brew's strength.

Drip brewing requires a careful balance of variables. Grind fineness, batch size, and other factors must work together precisely to ensure that hot water drenches the grounds for an exact amount of time. This does not mean you can't make great drip coffee; it just requires a more minute grind or formula changes.

Materials

Kettle

Stovetop

Fresh water, 6 ounces (180 ml) for every 2 tablespoons (10 g) whole bean coffee

Digital scale

Fresh coffee, 2 tablespoons (10 g) whole bean per 6 ounces (180 ml) water

Grinder set to medium-fine

Paper or mesh filter (see page 93 for recommendations)

Drip maker, one that makes the amount of coffee you like to drink

Thermometer, optional

< Manual drip brewing's advantage is in the hands of the hot water pourer. You can literally steer the stream to ensure all the grounds are thoroughly submerged by piping hot water. The foaming on the fresh-soaked grounds is a sign of roasting freshness.

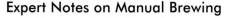

Expert Notes on Manual Brewing

Here are some tips for brewing manually:

- Time a batch. Pay attention to the moment the grounds get wet until the last drip of coffee enters the carafe. If the time exceeds seven minutes (including a one-minute break for initial grounds foaming and settling), coarsen your grind and repeat.

- Run water through bleached filters (which I recommend) before setting in the brewer to remove any possible chemicals used for whitening (usually hydrogen peroxide, not chlorine). This will prepare the filter for brewing and prevent even the slightest possibility that it will absorb your first coffee extracts.

- Watch the temperature. If you use a thermometer, pour water when it reads 200°F (90°C) instead of one minute off the boil.

- Examine the filter after brewing. The top of the grounds bed should look flat and wet, indicating that all of the grounds participated equally in the extraction process.

- Stir the drip coffee before serving the finished brew. The first extracts are stronger than the last.

- Compost the used coffee grounds and paper filters.

Instructions

1. Set the water kettle on high heat to boil.

2. Weigh the whole beans and grind medium-fine. Do not grind too fine.

3. Prewet the paper filter, fold the filter in half, and set it in the basket. Place the double fold (the thicker of the two sides) over the runnel (the channel on the brewer).

4. Add the grounds to the filter **(a)**. Shake the basket to settle the grounds, but never pack them.

5. Remove the boiling water from the heat and let it stand for 1 minute or until the water stops bubbling.

6. Slowly pour the water over the grounds in a circular motion **(b)**. Fresh roaster/fresh ground coffee will likely foam up (releasing carbon dioxide) and then settle back down. For better flavor extraction, allow this to occur before pouring more water.

7. Repeat until all the coffee is brewed.

8. Remove the filter and discard.

9. Stir the brew to mix together the strongest coffee, which comes through earliest, with the weaker coffee, which comes at the drip brew's end. Serve the coffee **(c)**.

Manual Drip Tutorial

Automatic Drip

Unlike manual drip, automatic drip features onboard water boiling and delivery over the grounds. In other words, this brewer does the heating for you, decides when the water is hot enough, and then dribbles it over your coffee grounds. From that point on, it's no different than the manual drip, with gravity pulling the water through the ground coffee and the brew falling from the filter into the carafe below.

Despite its name, automatic drip still requires the user to measure and grind coffee and have knowledge of the overall coffee-making process, particularly knowing how to tweak an automatic drip (see pages 102 for more information). Fully automatic machines are in development, but haven't arrived yet.

Materials

Digital scale

Fresh whole bean coffee, 2 tablespoons (10 g) per 6 ounces (180 ml) water

Grinder set to medium-fine

Automatic drip brewer (preferably one that brews a full batch in 6 minutes or less)

Fresh water, 6 ounces (180 ml) for every 2 tablespoons (10 g) whole bean coffee

Paper or metal filter (see page 93 for recommendations)

< Automatic drip brewers offer convenience and a sleek design for the modern kitchen.

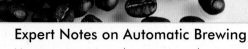

Expert Notes on Automatic Brewing

Here are some notes about automatic brews:

- Examine the grounds after brewing. All the grounds should appear damp, with no dry grounds present, and lie flat. This indicates an even, thorough soaking. If you see dry grounds, grind finer next time.

- Adjust the batch size until you get it right. For example, if the brewer takes longer than six minutes and the grounds are wet but didn't overflow, make a smaller batch next time.

- Grind coarser if the grounds basket over-flowed during brewing.

- Add water to the finished brew if the coffee is too strong.

- Use less ground coffee if the coffee retains some bitter notes.

- Check the brewer's temperature if the coffee is weak but contact time is six minutes. Wearing an oven mitt, hold a thermometer under the brewer's spray head (if you have a flexible thermometer, place it into the brew basket and run a full cycle). It should read between 190°F (88°C) and 205°F (96°C). If the temperature and timing are right and the grounds are getting soaked, but the coffee still ends up too strong or too weak, adjust the brew formula or move the grind one notch in either direction.

Instructions

1. Weigh whole bean or ground coffee. If using whole bean, grind medium-fine. Do not grind too fine.

2. Fill the machine's water compartment, usually up top, with cold water **(a)**.

3. Prewet the filter and insert it into the holder.

4. Add the grounds to the filter. Shake the basket to settle the grounds flat, but never pack them **(b)**.

5. Close the lid or insert the filter holder into the machine, depending on your model's design.

6. Turn the brewing switch on.

7. Time from the first drip until the last drip exits the filter. This should take 6 minutes maximum **(c)**.

8. Stir the finished brew in the carafe to mix earlier, stronger coffee with later, weaker extraction.

Automatic Drip Tutorial

Press Pot/French Press/Melior

We refer to this method as press pot, though it's also called the French press or the Melior. A drip coffee brewer (page 101) pours hot water down through grounds, and a vacuum brewer (described later in this chapter on page 113) shoots hot water up through grounds. The press works by keeping water around the grounds still—also known as steeping. This seems to produce a different extraction and flavor. No one knows whether the still water causes different oils to come forth or whether it just reacts differently and changes the taste. But almost everyone agrees that the press "just tastes different."

Many who evaluate coffees for a living claim the press comes closest of all methods to matching the cupping taste experience (see chapter 2, page 47 for more on cupping).

A press pot's plunger usually consists of a metal screen over a solid metal piece and a rod that screws into them, which allows you to drive the filter down through the hot brewed coffee. This gets threaded through a metal or plastic cap that fits over the glass cylinder. Most presses come preassembled and with simple instructions on dismantling and reassembling.

Materials

Kettle

Fresh water, 6 ounces (180 ml) for every
2 tablespoons (10 g) whole bean coffee

Stovetop

Glass or stainless-steel press pot, including metal filter assembly, usually attached to the lid (the plunger)

Digital scale

Grinder set to coarse

Fresh coffee, 2 tablespoons (10 g) ground per
6 ounces (180 ml) water

Kitchen timer or clock

Spoon

< The plunger on its top makes the French press easily recognizable.

Press Pot/French Press/
Melior (continued)

Expert Notes on Press Pot Brewing

Here are a few tips about press pot brewing:

- Do not stir press pot coffee after brewing to even out its strength. Instead, evenly distribute the coffee across serving cups. Pour a small amount into one cup, then into another, then into another. Repeat to put equal-strength coffee in each cup.

- Facilitate extraction by plunging the press up and down to agitate the grounds during steeping.

- Expect some grounds in every cup. It's part of the press experience and some aficionados like it. To reduce the amount, pour brewed coffee slowly.

- Brew small batches of press pot coffee if the press will likely sit out for a time. The press coffee cools rapidly, and there is no way to preserve the heat (unless you have an insulated metal model).

- Keep the filters clean. Instead of rinsing or placing the fully assembled plunger filter into the dishwasher, disassemble it each time. Grounds and hard-to-see oils accumulate quickly, particularly between the mesh filter and the hard metal plate that holds it in place, as well as in any crevices. You don't want so-called "seasoning" of these metal parts, so squeaky clean it is.

Instructions

1. Fill the kettle with appropriate volume of water. For example, for four 6-ounce (180 ml) cups, heat 3 cups (720 ml) of water plus an additional 8 ounces (240 ml) for scalding the press pot and evaporation. Heat on medium heat until it reaches a boil.

2. In the meantime, assemble the press plunger (if you have dismantled it for cleaning).

3. Grind 2 tablespoons (10 g) whole bean coffee coarsely for each 6-ounce cup (180 ml) and set aside.

4. Preheat the press pot by scalding it with 4 ounces (120 ml) hot water.

5. Swirl the water and then discard it.

6. Add the ground coffee to the empty pot **(a)**.

7. Pour about half of your hot water over the grounds **(b)**. With fresh coffee, foam will form and swell. Let the foam rise and fall **(c)**.

8. Set your timer to 4 minutes. Pour the remaining hot water into the pot.

9. Place the plunger cap on the cylinder. Depress the plunger just enough so that the top of the grounds are held under the water. Start the timer. Once each minute, agitate the grounds (by swirling, pressing the plunger up and down, or stirring) to prevent clumping and to ensure maximum extraction **(d)**.

10. At the 4-minute mark, slowly but firmly depress the plunger fully.

11. Pour the coffee slowly to keep sediment in the cups to a minimum **(e)** and evenly distribute it among the cups.

Press Pot/French Press/Melior Tutorial

Neapolitan Flip/Drip Maker

This unit consists of a water reservoir, a filter with screw top, and a carafe all in one neat, assembled package. The Neapolitan brewer is sometimes called a reversible drip, which explains its method. How does it work? Assemble the pieces and place the water-heating half (with spout upside down) on the heat. Once the water almost reaches boiling, turn the whole brewer upside down so it can function as a drip brewer.

Neapolitan brewers are often mistaken for stovetop espresso or Moka machines (which we discuss in chapter 6), but the only pressure in these machines is gravity. A hole in the side just above the water line counts on the fact that boiling water rises. The droplet it spits out signals you to flip. A combination of its stainless steel mesh filter and grounds held in a tight space throughout the brew give coffee brewed in a Neapolitan a richness, with some sediment, and a flavor profile akin to a press pot.

Materials

Three-piece brewer, consisting of water reservoir, coffee filter, and serving pitcher

Digital scale

Fresh whole bean coffee, 2 tablespoons (10 g) per 6 ounces (180 ml) water

Grinder set to percolator (coarse) grind

Fresh water, 6 ounces (180 ml) for every 2 tablespoons (10 g) whole bean coffee

Stovetop

Heat-safe glove or oven mitt

< A flip drip brewer works just like its name suggests: by heating the water to the start of boiling and flipping it over to allow the water to drip through a filter into the pitcher half. It is simple, and it results in a very rich, full-bodied couple of cups of coffee.

Flip/Drip, Coarse Grounds

The flip drip machine offers a powerful tasting cup, unusual considering its use of coarse grinds and its fairly quick contact time. If coffee comes out too strong or has more than a couple of grounds, grind even coarser. Some texts about this method specify fine grind, but I've found that coarse works far better.

Instructions

1. Disassemble the brewer.

2. Measure out whole bean or ground coffee. If using whole bean, grind coarse.

3. Unscrew the cap on the filter section and fill with 2 tablespoons (10 g) coarse ground coffee **(a)**. Smooth the grounds so they lie flat, but do not press them down. Replace the cap.

4. Fill the brewer's water reservoir up to one-quarter inch (6.35 mm) from the small hole **(b)**. Allowing this clearance will compensate for water expansion.

5. Place the filter inside the reservoir **(c)**.

6. Connect the brewer's serving pitcher half (the part with the spout) to the other half **(d)**.

7. Place the assembled brewer on a burner **(e)**. On a gas stove, don't allow the flame to extend beyond the brewer's width. Instead, compensate by centering it on a portion of the flame.

8. When a droplet of water appears at the small hole, turn off the heat. Wearing an oven mitt, grab the handle and flip over the unit **(f, g, h)**. Place it back on the stove.

9. When the bottom half of the brewer fills, your coffee is ready.

Neopolitan Flip/Drip Maker Tutorial

Vacuum Brewer

The vacuum brewer, which resembles an hourglass, consists of a water reservoir, a filter, and a brewing upper bowl with a long stem. It involves heating water in its bottom half, shooting hot water up through the grounds, and agitating grounds during contact time. A vacuum created as the water bowl cools draws filtered, brewed coffee into the lower bowl. The top half is removed before serving the pot of coffee. It is unique among brewing styles because water doesn't touch the grounds until it is hot enough to brew adequately. Agitation during extraction ensures thorough mixing of grounds and water. The vacuum's pull efficiently drains the finished brew from the grounds.

It does have a couple of trouble spots. The glass upper bowl stems are prone to snapping when hot, which is when you're most likely to place stress on them. Also, vacuum brewing is relatively high-maintenance, is messy, and requires significant cleanup and manual timing.

That said, it uses the finest grind of any non-espresso method. Some ancient supermarket coffee grinders have a "glass," "vacuum," or "fine" setting designed for the vacuum's relatively short contact time. Once you learn and master this method, it's easy to get hooked. It may become your favorite, particularly for entertaining.

Materials

Three-piece vacuum maker, consisting of upper bowl, bottom bowl, and filter

Fresh water, 8 ounces (240 ml) for every 2 tablespoons (10 g) whole bean coffee

Digital scale

Fresh whole bean coffee, 2 tablespoons (10 g) whole bean per 8 ounces (240 ml) water

Grinder set to fine

Stovetop or heating element

Spoon

Kitchen timer or clock

Heat-safe gloves

< The glass vacuum brewer has a lot going for it. It is beautiful to watch, does a thorough job extracting oils from the grounds, and delivers just about as hot a cup of coffee as possible. It just might become a favorite brewer, if you're willing to take the time and attention.

Vacuum Brewer (continued)

Instructions

1. Fill the lower bowl with carefully measured cold water. For this method, use 8 ounces (240 ml) of water per 2 tablespoons (10 g) of finely ground coffee to make up for water lost during brewing.

2. Measure out whole bean or ground coffee. If using whole bean, grind coarse.

3. Insert the filter into the upper bowl (a). Any type of vacuum filters (glass, ceramic, or metal) will produce a high-quality brew.

4. Add approximately 2 tablespoons (10 g) finely ground coffee per 8 ounces (240 ml) of water (b).

5. Place the lower bowl on the heat source on medium heat. Let the water come to a boil and then place the upper bowl snugly inside the lower bowl (c, d). Steam should develop in the lower bowl, which then forces water to rise through the tube and filter into the upper bowl, where it mixes with the coffee. Keep a spoon nearby to gently stir the grounds and facilitate mixing (e).

6. When most of the water has risen into the upper bowl, start a timer. A small amount of boiling water should remain in the lower bowl (f).

7. Lower the heat just enough to keep the lower bowl water boiling.

8. After 1 minute, remove the entire brewer from the heat source, ideally using heat-safe gloves (g). Place the brewer on a trivet or heat-resistant surface. The sudden temperature drop in the lower bowl should start the vacuum process, during which the freshly brewed coffee is drawn down through the filter tube and into the lower bowl.

9. Once most of the coffee has returned to the lower bowl, listen for a gentle bubbling. This indicates that the vacuum has drawn every bit of coffee flavor from the grounds. (Examining the spent grounds should reveal that they are almost dry.)

10. Carefully separate the two bowls. Some vacuum brewers come with a cooling stand (h). If yours does not, lay the upper bowl on its side in the sink until you are ready to clean it.

11. Stir the coffee in the lower bowl and serve.

Vacuum Brewer Tutorial

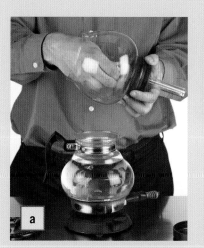

a

b

c

d

e

f

g

h

Percolator

A percolator consists of a water boiling vessel and a tubed, inserted filtering device that holds ground coffee. In this method, boiling water rises up through the tube and sprays over the grounds. The water travels down through the grounds and through a bottom screen where it lands back in the boiling vessel. It is boiled again and travels the same path. This repeats for six to eight minutes or until your desired strength is reached. Many coffee aficionados "accept" only the first boil, because all succeeding contact boils the coffee. However, a manual percolator operated with a gentle boil can produce strong coffee with minimal bitterness. Note, electric models may or may not reduce heat during brewing. Models that do not reduce heat will cause more bitterness.

Materials

Percolator

Fresh water, 6 ounces (180 ml) for every 2 tablespoons (10 g) whole bean coffee

Digital scale

Fresh whole bean coffee, 2 tablespoons (10 g) whole bean per 6 ounces (180 ml) water

Grinder set to course

Stovetop or electric outlet

Timer

< The percolator is accused of violating the number one rule of brewing in that it boils the coffee during brewing. Using a low flame (on a gas range) and a manual percolator, it is possible to achieve a low boil, with deliciously strong results

Percolator (continued)

Expert Notes on Percolator

Here are some tips on using a percolator:

- Use the lowest possible heat setting once the water boils to a simmer to reduce bitterness.

- Stop heating at eight minutes, otherwise you may accentuate bitterness. Remember, the coffee will continue heating after you turn off your heat source. A little goes a long way.

- Try light roasted coffees for percolators. Low-acidity coffees such as Brazilian and Sumatran varieties take advantage of the percolator's high-extraction temperatures. Higher-acidity coffees brewed in percolators can end up tasting too sharp.

Instructions

1. Disassemble the percolator.

2. Fill the water boiling vessel with the appropriate volume of water **(a)**. Do not fill above the bottom of the inserted filter.

3. Measure out whole bean or ground coffee. If using whole bean, grind coarse.

4. Remove the top grate of the filter and add to the filter basket approximately 2 tablespoons (10 g) coarse ground coffee per 6 ounces (180 ml) water **(b)**. Replace the top grate **(c)**.

5. Place the percolator on medium heat or plug in electric model. Set a timer for 6 to 8 minutes.

6. When the water starts boiling (perking), lower the heat to just enough to maintain simmer.

7. Start the timer. Now the machine takes over. The boiling water rises up through the tube, sprays the grounds, and drips through the grinds back into the boiling vessel. This process repeats for approximately 8 minutes.

8. After 6 to 8 minutes (depending on your desired taste), remove the percolator from your heat source **(d)**.

9. Keep it warm on very low heat. Serve the coffee immediately.

Percolator Tutorial

Ibrik/Turkish/Greek Method

The ibrik method, also called Turkish or Greek, consists of tossing pulverized coffee grounds into a vessel with water. The water is boiled with the grounds multiple times. There is no filter. The grounds settle, so carefully pouring the coffee is the only way to reduce the amount that ends up in cups. Some in the coffee industry consider the careful pouring part of ibrik coffee making an art form. To some, ibrik represents coffee brewing at its oldest and most basic form.

Traditionally, ibrik coffee is served sugarless at funerals or unhappy occasions and with extra sugar at weddings and other festivities. Also, in some Arabic countries, serving someone the coffee without any foam signifies "losing face" because the foam is considered the coffee's face. Be careful. If you don't divide the foam equally, you could send the wrong message.

Materials

Ibrik coffee maker (copper)

Fresh water, 3 ounces (90 ml) for every 2 tablespoons (10 g) whole bean coffee

Digital scale

Fresh dark roasted whole bean coffee, 2 tablespoons (10 g) ground superfine

Mortar and pestle "grinder" or a true ibrik grinder (which looks like a pepper mill)

Sugar

Stovetop or other heat source

1- to 3-ounce (30 to 90 ml) demitasse cups

Spoon

< Ibrik coffee is considered real coffee by much of the world. Properly made, it can be a powerful, aromatic taste sensation. Part of its art is in its creation, and its rituals are as rich as its taste.

Ibrik/Turkish/Greek Method (continued)

Expert Notes on Ibrik

Here are some tips for ibrik brewing

- To minimize the grounds in a cup, don't constantly stir; a little stirring goes a long way.

- Pour ibrik coffee very slowly, as most of the grounds will have sunk to the bottom. The ibrik coffee pot automatically hangs at a forty-five degree angle. Try pouring at that angle as well.

- Add a pinch of cardamom for flavoring. This is perhaps the earliest known form of flavored coffee. Also try orange-blossom water. Add more or less to your preference.

Instructions

1. Place 3 ounces (90 ml) of water into the ibrik **(a)**.

2. Add 2 tablespoons (10 g) of powder ground coffee **(b)**.

3. Add 1 tablespoon (12 g) of sugar per demitasse **(c)**. Never fill an ibrik more than half full. It will foam up during boiling and could overflow.

4. Put the ibrik on medium heat and bring mixture to a boil **(d)**. Once it boils, lower the heat so it won't overflow. Also, gentle heat produces a milder cup. Let it sit for 1 or 2 minutes.

5. Once the coffee stops boiling, repeat the process, bringing it to a boil twice more, reducing heat immediately upon boiling.

6. As it reaches a boil its third and final time (and likely, as the foam nears the top of the ibrik's neck, in spite of our precautions), remove the ibrik from the heat.

7. Pour carefully into prewarmed demitasse cups. Divide the foam between the cups using a spoon.

Ibrik/Turkish/Greek Method Tutorial

Open Pot/Cowboy/ Campfire Coffee

Open pot coffee means boiling or almost-boiling water and tossing in grounds. This is coffee brewing at its most basic. It requires nothing but a pan (and coffee and water, of course). It's good for making large batches of coffee. At one time, a church that wanted to make coffee for its social used this method.

Materials

Pan, deep enough to hold a decent amount of water with no overflow risk

2½ gallons (9.5 L) water

Stovetop or other heat source

1 pound (455 g) whole bean coffee, 2 tablespoons (10 g) per 6 ounces (180 ml) water

Grinder set to coarse

Filter bag (made from any kind of tight weave, such as a sock or a sugar sack)

String, to tie filter bag closed

Timer

CAN'T HANDLE THE SOCK?

If the thought of using a sock turns your stomach, don't use one. Instead, put the grinds directly into the water and at the eight-minute mark, just after removing pan from heat, use a strainer to remove them.

Instructions

1. Measure and fill open the pan with water.

2. Place on high heat. Once the water boils, lower the heat to bring it just under boiling, recognizable by pea-sized bubbles.

3. Grind the coffee beans. Use 2 tablespoons (10 g) of coffee per 6 ounces (180 ml) of water. For large crowds, use 1 pound (455 g) of coffee to 2½ gallons (9.5 L) of water.

4. Place the grounds into a filter (**a**). Tie a string around the filter but leave plenty of room for the grounds to swell (**b**).

5. Shut off the heat. Drop the grounds into the water and begin timing.

6. After 10 to 15 minutes, remove the filter (**c**) and serve the coffee with a ladle.

Open Pot/Cowboy/Campfire Tutorial

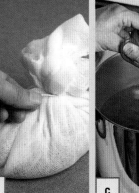

< Open pot coffee is boiled in the stovetop and served with a ladle.

6 ESPRESSO

ESPRESSO is a highly concentrated coffee drink, the basis of a litany of beverages found in cafés all around the world. Some people mispronounce it "ex-presso"—an almost intuitive mistake considering the quick process to make the drink.

Making espresso requires a dedicated espresso machine, most of which consist of a chassis with a boiler. Once the water gets hot enough, a pump allows it to flow into a metal device called a head or group, which contains packed grounds. The pressure from the machine then forces the water through the grounds, extracting the precious coffee oils in seconds. The liquid coffee excretes through a bottom spout in the head.

Normally, espresso is served in one- or two-ounce (30 or 60 ml) amounts depending on the machine's head or group size. The industry refers to espresso in one-ounce (30 ml) form as a shot. So when a customer requests a triple-shot espresso, assume the order calls for three ounces (90 ml) of espresso.

Although some consider espresso the strongest-tasting coffee (see "Ibrik," chapter 5, page 121, for a counter-argument), paradoxically, it has the lowest caffeine content by serving (though not volume). People who claim to be "high" on espresso after drinking a shot or two may be experiencing what's known as the placebo effect—they think the espresso's caffeine will affect them, so it does. Perhaps the fact that it's easy to drink a high volume of espresso, especially when it's buried in mounds of froth and made from higher caffeine Robusta coffee beans, might offer an explanation.

In this chapter, you will learn the following:

- What factors go into making the perfect espresso

- How to select the appropriate grind for your espresso maker

- What extraction time, tamping pressure, and espresso bitterness mean

- How to differentiate and select an espresso maker

- How to pull the perfect espresso shot

< The espresso was invented for its brevity, but has stayed due to its powerful taste and versatility. Here is a perfect espresso shot in the making, showing off its twin "mouse's tail" drips.

The History and Science of Espresso

Italy's communist government originally embraced espresso as an attempt to shorten the world-renowned Italian coffee break. Giovanni Achille Gaggia actually invented espresso. In his Milan coffee shop, Gaggia patented a piston, which he attached to existing coffee brewing machines to try to reduce the coffee's bitterness. In 1947, after eight years, he succeeded.

In many ways, it was the most significant coffee-brewing development of the modern age. In the 1960s, espresso took off around the world, as American tourists tasted the drink in Italy and brought it home, and films started showing movie stars drinking it.

For home aficionados, espresso is complex and anything but efficient. But to its fans, it is the holy grail of coffee preparation, a coffee obsessive's dream hobby. It has all the maddening, glorifying manic-depressive experience of a great love affair. Espresso mastery demonstrates the hobbyist's expertise (and madness) to friends and relatives. Part of espresso's allure is, no doubt, its preparation. With practice and skill, you'll get better at making espresso. One day, your espresso machine may even become your first choice.

Most coffee-making methods depend on gravity or steeping, but espresso is a high-pressure extraction method, which means you can produce a strong-tasting beverage quickly. Small variations in grind fineness, timing, or water pressure result in significant flavor differences. Serious espresso hobbyists thoroughly research their process. They want to know the pressure (measured in bars—the higher the number, the greater the pressure) and water temperature. If a drip machine takes thirty seconds to reach ideal brew temperature, it won't ruin the cup; thirty seconds is the *total* brewing time for an espresso.

What Defines a Great Espresso?

You must consider many factors when attempting to create a great espresso.

Grind

Nearly everything comes down to the grind with espresso. No two espresso machines or grinders are perfectly alike. I cannot stress enough the importance of matching the correct grind with a given machine. Preground coffee is especially problematic for home espresso making. Though preground is usually fresh enough for home drip methods, it will likely never be fresh enough for espresso and will almost certainly result in a lackluster shot. (See the section later in the chapter on page 136 about selecting the appropriate grind for your espresso machine.)

Each day, check and calibrate the espresso's grind before making consumable shots. Humidity variation from one day to the next affects espresso. Also, if the grind is too coarse, the water will flow through the head too quickly, resulting in a weak, thin shot. If it's too fine, the water will flow too slowly through the head, and a bitter, thick coffee will result. At each session, try different grind settings to discover which creates the perfect grind consistency for your machine.

Taste

Espresso tastes distinct from other coffee brewing methods. It is so different that it often benefits from its own blends and roasts. Also, because of its on-site creation moments before serving, rather than sitting for hours on a burner, it's guaranteed to taste fresh.

A well-made espresso shot should taste almost tangy. It is definitely more bitter than traditional filtered coffee, so expect some bitterness. Most consumers do not drink straight espresso, but they

If the grind is too coarse, the espresso shot flows too fast.

If the grind is too fine, the espresso shot barely drips out.

drink latte beverages that contain espresso. The sweetness of the milk in these drinks nicely offsets any bitterness.

Connoisseurs who do have straight espresso limit their bitterness by drinking blended espressos or origin coffees such as Brazil's and carefully optimizing the brewing process. Of course, you want a little bitterness, but not too much. Espresso mavens claim that they can deliver smooth, silky, and even sweet shots. If you only drink properly made drip coffee, your first espresso may be a shock, especially if you expect sweetness.

Roast is certainly a factor in bitterness. For less bitter espresso, experiment with lighter roast coffees. A middle ground exists between a light roast's sharp acidity and a dark roast's bitterness amidst its caramel notes. Someone who drinks espresso straight may find satisfaction there.

Foam

In addition to its taste, a successful espresso shot is judged visually, primarily by the layer of brownish foam on top called the crema (pronounced Krem-uh)—espresso's equivalent to a diamond ring's stone. It should appear strong and beautiful. The crema also indicates a viscosity, or creaminess, of the entire beverage, part of its appeal.

If purchasing an espresso machine, keep in mind the following industry specs:

- 200°F (93°C) water temperature.

- Seven grams (¼ oz) fine ground coffee per one-ounce (30 ml) serving. Most machines come with their own appropriately sized spoons.

- Nine atmospheres pressure (132 pounds per square inch). This indicates how much pressure the manufacturer of the machine has put into the water as it goes through the coffee.

- Twenty-five to thirty seconds of extraction time

As you become more immersed as an espresso hobbyist, you will no doubt find passionate enthusiasts who prefer different variables and manufacturers that cater to different experiences. Some variables, such as extraction time, are user-controlled. In other words, play with them until they suit your taste.

The crema indicates the espresso's strength, beauty, and creaminess.

Tamping the Grounds

Proper tamping of the grounds (leveling them in the head or group) will make or break a shot, even if you have the correct grind. Here's how to do it:

1. Fill the group (or head) with coffee. Level off the grinds with your hand **(a)**.

2. Grasp the top of the tamper firmly **(b)**. Rotate your arm inward **(c)**.

3. Begin tamping. Apply even pressure to pack the grounds.

4. Using your finger, polish the edges of the group to remove all excess grounds **(d)**.

5. Inspect the coffee to make sure it is smooth **(e)**.

6. Place the group sideways into the machine and turn the handle to seat it properly **(f)**.

Tamping the Grounds Tutorial

Expert Notes from a Barista

Espresso-making—and its terminology—can be confusing, so we asked a barista at a well-known retail espresso chain to offer some tips about three issues: extraction time, tamping, and bitterness.

Extraction time: This is simply the amount of time it takes for the water to filter through the grinds and into the cup. Some take only twenty seconds. Others require thirty seconds. Experiment to determine how long works for each coffee and let your taste buds be your guide. Machine, grind, and bean quality will likely play a much larger role than extraction time alone.

Tamping pressure: Tamping is the process of leveling the coffee in the filter head. To do this, use a tool called a tamper. Some espresso makers suggest tamping at forty pounds of pressure. In other words, the force you use puts about forty pounds of pressure on the coffee. Tamping at twenty pounds is low, but it likely won't make or break your espresso outcome. It takes practice to understand the force necessary to tamp at certain pressures. Be consistent with your tamping because identical grinds tamped at two different pressures will taste different. Try not to overtamp (e.g., with fifty pounds or more).

Espresso bitterness: In a quality shot, very little bitterness should come through (though you do want some). Sweetness is more frequently one of the most apparent qualities. That said, if a shot tastes too bitter, it likely is. Throw it away.

Espresso Maker Guide

Once the exclusive province of wealthy urbanites and bad–credit risk over-reachers, espresso machines are now available at most price levels. European manufacturers have been particularly innovative in developing inexpensive mechanisms that deliver brewing pressure without costly industrial-grade pumps. Some new entry-level machines do a good job of delivering a palatable one-ounce (30 ml) shot or serving of espresso. The trouble is that the enemy of good is great, and for great espresso, none but the highest-end consumer machines (some might even call them "pro-sumer" machines) can deliver the absolute best espresso.

The following is an espresso machines rough guide in ascending order. I do not endorse any one brand or model, as they change often.

Stovetop Moka

This machine is really a hybrid espresso/drip machine. It doesn't generate enough pressure to develop a crema, but it often rivals low-end espresso machines, at a fraction of the cost. Something about them says "artsy" and "non-conformist" and that the owner is an individualist. It even says you don't like to pay money for appliances that don't make any better coffee.

Advantages: Low cost, good flavor, required bitterness

Disadvantages: Cleanup, no crema, no milk foam

Materials

Three piece Moka maker

1 cup (240 ml) water

7 grams (¼ oz) coarse ground coffee for a 1-ounce (30 ml) single shot or 14 grams (½ oz) for a double (two 1-ounce [30 ml] shots)

Stovetop or other heat source

Instructions

1. Fill the bottom of the maker with water to just under the steam-release hole **(a)**.

2. Fill the filter with coarse ground coffee **(b)**.

3. With your hand, smooth the top of the coffee in the filter. Don't try to press the coffee but smooth it instead. This is called polishing the dose **(c)**.

4. Screw on the top half of brewer.

5. Turn the stovetop on low flame and brew until water comes out of the steam-release hole **(d)**.

6. Serve the Moka immediately **(e)**.

< The stovetop Moka is a hybrid brewer that brews coffee that sits somewhere between true espresso and strong drip coffee. For many, it is an almost perfect compromise in the cup, and it is easy to make.

Stovetop Moka Tutorial

Stovetop Espresso Machines

What's the difference between a Moka and a stovetop espresso machine? Oh, it's about 30 dollars. Sorry for the bad joke, but really, there often isn't much difference. A well-designed stovetop espresso machine will produce a bit more pressure—and subsequently more crema—although nothing like the best shot.

Advantages: Reasonable cost, slightly better espresso character than a stovetop Moka

Disadvantages: Cleanup, little or no crema, no milk foam

Electric Steam Espresso

This machine looks like a home espresso machine should. It has a steam wand, a device that's not used to brew coffee but rather to steam and froth milk. Because the majority of people drink espresso in cappuccinos and lattes, you may consider getting one of these if you're on a budget (and don't really want espresso as much as a strong milk-frothed café latte drink). The coffee can taste quite good, but as espresso, it lacks the tight foam of a well-made commercial shot and the creamy tight bubbles associated with the best cappuccino or latte art.

Advantages: Decent retail price, some companies' innovations produce surprisingly good near-espresso

Disadvantages: The majority of steam machines overextract and make bitter espresso-style drinks, okay milk foam

Pump Espresso Machines

Pump machines are the entry point for most home espresso hobbyists. The invention of the pump, which allows pressurization then heating of cold water, created the commercial espresso industry. Some very fine consumer or "pro-sumer" pump espresso machine models exist out there. Some challenge the finest commercial machines and will certainly outperform a local chain's café, especially if you buy the best espresso beans, learn to grind, and make the coffee to maximum potential. Many of these machines come with pounds per square inch ratings, which will indicate how much pressure the machine uses to force water through the grounds (and which results in crema).

Advantages: Gives many hobbyists the epiphany moment in their hobby's gestation (in other words, it's good)

Disadvantage: High price

Manual Piston Machines

The piston features a long handle on top. The idea is to build up pressure and then very gently release it and using your own intuition and skill to manually control the shot's creation. It is the ultimate machine for the control freak. It's not easy to use and often features no milk frothing or steaming capability. But in the right hands, it can produce a great espresso.

Advantages: Makes great espresso when you know how to use it, workable

Disadvantages: Not for the faint-hearted, requires skill, inconsistent frothing

Automatic Piston Machines

This is the type of machine about which most espresso hobbyists dream. Instead of using a manual handle, like the machine described previously, this machine's piston lives inside and has enough pressure to make perfect milk. A professional barista will have this type of machine at home. Don't confuse these machines with fully automatic models.

Advantages: With practice, makes drinks like the cafés do

Disadvantages: Requires time (to learn how to use it) and money (to purchase it)

Electric steam espresso machine

Pump espresso machine

PODS

Espresso pods are single serving preground espresso coffee clothed in filter paper packets. To use a pod, simply drop it into your espresso filter holder (group) and fire away. Pods remove the need to grind, an obstacle for many espresso/latte drinkers, and increase the ease of making home espresso. The espresso coffee industry spent much time and money improving packaging to keep the product fresh. Pods do not equal the best fresh roasted and ground espresso, but they offer a decent option when convenience outranks perfection. It is important to note that there are pod brewing methods that aren't espresso but rather adaptations of the drip method.

Manual piston machine. In the piston's long handle, pressure builds up until you release it

Espresso Grinders and Grinding

Make no mistake about it, espresso requires very fine, exact, and repeatable grinds, even some of the forgiving consumer designs. In tests comparing a top-rated burr coffee grinder, a good consumer espresso grinder, and a commercial espresso grinder, the espresso shot flavor differences were profound and unsubtle. Try this yourself. You'll certainly be able to tell the difference. Conclusion: Expect to put as much or more emphasis and budget into your espresso grinder as you do your machine.

Presently, none of the home grinders I have tested for regular or drip coffee really extends its performance to include espresso. Why? Grinders are optimized to a range of grinds, but espresso falls outside of this range. Its thirty-second contact time is such a narrow window of opportunity that the need for exact particle-sized grounds increases exponentially. Most espresso hobbyists have a dedicated espresso grinder with burrs especially optimized for fine grinds.

In terms of roast, technically, you can use any coffee in an espresso maker. But most experts agree that espresso's pressure seems to overemphasize light roasted coffee's acidity. Therefore, darker and less acidic roasts, origins, and blends work best for espresso. Light-roasted Kenya AA, stellar in a vacuum brewer, may taste harsh in an espresso machine. A Brazilian low-acid darker roast coffee that may taste dull in a press pot just might make a terrific espresso shot.

And what kind of grinds work best for which machines? Here's a quick rundown:

Coarse Grinds

Works for: Stovetop Moka machines, stovetop espresso machines, and electric steam machines

Grind type: Remember your childhood sandbox? These machines like a fine but grittier grind that still contains some powder. However, more than half of the grind should be distinct particles. You're off with your grind if the machine clogs up or runs too fast. Beyond this, fine tune it by time.

Fine Grinds

Works for: Commercial, pump espresso machines, and manual and automatic pistons

Grind type: Coarser than flour (maybe whole grain flour) and just a baby step coarser than Turkish ibrik (see chapter 5, "Brewing," for more about ibrik)—in other words, very fine grinds. These high-pressure machines like to force their water through these fine grinds.

THE HUMIDITY FACTOR

As humidity increases, coarsen up your grind to compensate. During spring and summer, go a notch coarser to prevent your coffee from tasting overextracted. Seattle café owner David Schomer wrote in his book *Espresso Coffee: Professional Techniques* of having an espresso machine stop suddenly due to an unexpected humidity increase after he'd calibrated his grinder—just minutes before—in drier weather. This may be a subtle or dramatic effect, but it shows the importance of the grind. Lesson: Prepare to make adjustments for climate changes.

A perfect shot can easily be two perfect shots. Many espresso enthusiasts quickly realize with the same effort, they can double their output, either making a larger beverage for themselves or one to share.

Pulling the Perfect Shot

A properly made espresso shot has that head of natural foam we mentioned earlier called crema, what's considered the shot's visual signature. Crema is composed of tiny carbon dioxide bubbles made from the water forcing itself through the narrow crevices around tightly packed grounds.

Now that you know what's required for an espresso shot, here's how to make one. You should know that perfecting the espresso shot takes a lifetime for the espresso enthusiast. It is relatively easy to make any old espresso shot, but making a great one requires trial and error. Fortunately, the rewards of such dedication are quite tasty.

Making Multiple Shots
Home espresso machines feature smaller than commercial-size boilers and usually require recovery time between shots. For one or two people, this is unlikely to be a factor, but you may disappoint those half-dozen relatives at a holiday dinner. Know your maker's requirement.

If your espresso machine offers the option to make two shots at a time, use it whenever guests are around. It's easier on the machine because it uses its heating capacity more efficiently. Heating up water more frequently takes more power than heating a larger quantity of water less frequently.

Materials

Maker of your choice

Soft or softened water (< 100 parts per million)

Espresso-grind coffee, 7 grams (¼ oz) for a 1-ounce (30 ml) single shot or 14 grams (½ oz) for a double (two 1-ounce [30 ml] shots)

Espresso grinder

Tamper

Prewarmed 1-ounce (30 ml) shot glasses

Espresso Troubleshooting Guide

This is a quick reference sheet for espresso-related troubleshooting.

PROBLEM	SOLUTION
Weak flavor	Grind finer, tamp more firmly
Bitter taste	Grind coarser, pack grounds looser, change blends to a lighter roast coffee, back flush detergent left in machine
Burnt grounds taste	Wait to place portafilter in machine until just before brewing, as the machine's heat can transfer to the grounds
Inconsistency in shots (for example, first shot is strong, the next is weak)	Increase recovery time between shots
Espresso pour comes too quickly (< 30 seconds)	Grind finer, pack grounds tighter
Drip too slow (even after checking grind)	Delime or remove minerals from the machine
No crema or thin crema	Check coffee's freshness, grind finer, pack ground tighter
Cappuccino/latte foam runny or too loose	Use milk with higher fat content

Expert Notes on Pulling an Espresso Shot

Here are some tips for pulling a shot of espresso:

- Check your machine every day (or at least before every use). Experienced baristas daily spend from ten minutes to a half hour setting up their machines.

- Expect to change your grind. Baristas know that their grinds will change due to atmospheric condition changes. Ground coffee attracts moisture and can literally swell, which can slow or even stop the espresso extraction. The only solution is to grind more coffee more coarsely.

- Don't grind too much espresso at once. Fine ground coffee loses its freshness, aroma, and flavor within minutes after grinding. Grind just a little more than you need. (If you run your grinder empty, the last grounds will be too coarse.)

- Empty your grinder each day after use. Grounds that stay in the grinder overnight will get stale.

- Enjoy espresso immediately after brewing. Unlike drip coffee, which can sit for up to thirty minutes and still taste fresh, espresso drinks depend on their short-lived foam and heat. Even slow-sipping espresso connoisseurs want a just-made shot to start. The same is true for lattes, cappuccinos, and other espresso-based beverages.

- Follow the Italian ristretto method by erring on the side of slightly shorter shots. In general, with coffee, best results come from underextraction rather than overextraction. I suggest this rather than longer (lungo) pulls, which result in whitish foam and more acidity. Lungo espressos save money for large operations. But for small scale "at home" operations, it doesn't provide the same benefit. Use more coffee for strength, not longer pull times.

- Use more than seven grams per shot if stronger espresso tempts you.

For Water, Think Low— Not No—Minerals

Use water with low mineral content when possible. Espresso machines are so prone to mineral buildup that the guidelines for other brewers don't apply. Try a reverse osmosis water purifier, which removes approximately ninety-eight percent of minerals from water. Even salt-softened water can work. Don't worry about minerals prolonging contact time, as in with drip brewing. The forced pressure of the water through the grounds eliminates this concern. Distilled water, in my opinion, is still not appropriate. Think low, not no minerals.

< A perfect shot can easily be two perfect shots. Many espresso enthusiasts quickly realize with the same effort, they can double their output, either making a larger beverage for themselves or one to share.

Pulling the Perfect Shot (continued)

Instructions

1. Fill the tank with softened water up to your unit's fill line.

2. Turn on to preheat the machine. Espresso machines must warm up to function properly.

3. Place metal screened filter, called a portafilter, into the metal receptacle located under a sill positioned over where you place your shot glass or cup **(a)**. This receptacle is called a group. Many machines come with double-size portafilters featuring two exit spouts, designed to make two shots at once. This comes in handy. Many of us regularly make two shots. In fact, I always do, not only for a more powerful cup or for two people but because viewing multiple shots allows me to better analyze how well I've set the grind.

4. Make a shot using no coffee, running hot water only through your portafilter while it's in the machine. This is important to bring all the parts up to temperature.

5. Grind a small amount of coffee, a bit more than you need, in a grinder that features click stops for fine adjustment.

6. Remove the head from the machine and place the grounds in the espresso machine's filter.

7. Tamp the grounds firmly **(b)**. Repeat twice more (for a total of three times) to make sure the grounds are tightly packed. Brush loose grounds from the group's lip. This procedure is called polishing the shot. Some home machines are designed for less-tight tamping, but unless this is specified in the instructions, use a tight tamp.

8. Place the filter into the machine above the cup with a twist to ensure a correct, tight fit **(c)**.

9. Press the "on" or "brew" button to make your first (or seasoning) shot using coffee. Discard it immediately without analyzing for grind. It is simply to season the filter.

10. Grind more coffee and refill the portafilter. Place it in the machine.

11. Press the "on" or "brew" button and time this shot. It should take 25 to 30 seconds to make a 1-ounce (30 ml) shot. Most espresso shot glasses have marks that say when. In other words, they show when 1 ounce (30 ml) has come through. An automatic machine may automatically stop.

12. Observe the coffee's drip as it falls into the glass. It should not fall straight but have a slight curve and bulge. Baristas call a correctly falling shot a *mouse's tail*. Does yours look like a mouse's tail? **(d)**

13. Observe the shot. It should be a rich golden color with no holes and a nice head of foam or crema on top **(e)**.

14. Taste it. Is it flat? Bitter? If it took less than 20 seconds, it will likely be thin, weak, and flat tasting. If it took more than 30 seconds, it will likely be thick, strong, and bitter tasting.

15. Grind some more coffee and adjust your shot. To prolong the espresso shot's duration, grind finer. To speed it up, grind coarser. Expect to repeat this process several times before you make a shot that will impress a friend or your own taste buds.

Pulling the Perfect Shot Tutorial

a

b

c

d

e

7

COFFEE SERVING AND RECIPES

YOU'VE gone to a ton of effort to make the best coffee possible. Now it's time to serve. The reality is that presentation and serving can add or detract from taste. There are ideal temperatures at which to serve and enjoy coffee and plenty of ways to maximize taste. It means paying attention to details and learning different coffee recipes, but it's worth it.

So much coffee consumption happens before, during, and after food. But which foods go best with which coffees? What's the best use for cream and sugar?

By the end of this chapter, you'll know how to do the following:

- Pair foods with coffees

- Use cream and sugar to enhance rather than mask coffee's flavor

- Create a litany of coffee cocktails and after-dinner coffee cordials

And that will complete your education as a coffee entertainer. Let's drink!

< Coffee service: thermal carafe, coffee mug and saucer, sugar, and cream.

Coffee Presentation and Serving Equipment

Brewed coffee is a volatile liquid; it cools and evaporates quickly. For best results, drink coffee immediately after brewing. If you can't drink it right away, place it in a vessel that keeps it hot and preserves as much flavor as possible. Because coffee flavor deteriorates quickly, give storage some thought so you can enjoy more than one cup.

Warming Plates and Thermal Carafes

The earliest coffee drinkers kept their serving vessels warm by lighting a flame underneath. Modern automatic drip makers feature a heated plate on which the serving carafe sits. This method does a credible job of keeping the coffee hot and preserving its flavor. Heat rises, and usually the carafe's non-airtight lid allows for steam and brew evaporation—but not the coffee's heat—to escape. It can reliably keep coffee hot for about twenty minutes. Plus, the glass vessel is usually easy to clean after brewing.

Thermal carafes came about during the early twentieth century. They work on the theory that the substance being stored provides its own best heat. The vessel doesn't add heat but simply insulates the heat already being produced. The advantage of these thermal carafes is that they spread heat evenly throughout the brew, keeping it warm for up to an hour with no discernible flavor loss. On the flip side, they don't keep the coffee as hot as when initially brewed and they are often difficult to clean.

Recommendation: If you typically drink your coffee within a half hour of brewing it, a warming plate is fine and its carafe more easily kept clean. If the coffee will sit for up to an hour after brewing, a thermal carafe is a better choice.

Coffee To Go

Even the most refined coffee drinkers need to buy coffee on the go sometimes. Keep in mind that the material of the to-go cup may affect the coffee's flavor profile. Coffee to go tastes best in the wax-coated, temperature-resistant paper cups. Paper cups offer the extra advantage of being recyclable. Styrofoam is the less desirable choice. Styrofoam is made of a material called polystyrene. The styrene in this compound may leach out into the hot coffee, as much as 0.025 percent. This is enough for some coffee drinkers to notice both an off aroma and taste. Since styrene is fat soluble, even more could leach into beverages containing cream or whole milk. If you must get your coffee to go in Styrofoam, never microwave it to re-heat it, as it may cause even more styrene to migrate into the coffee.

Coffee and Food

Ever wonder why cafés and coffeehouses all serve high-carbohydrate rolls and doughnuts? The high fat content in bready foods nicely counters the high acidity in coffee. After the widespread growth of dark roasts in the 1990s, some coffee industry experts claimed that light roasts better matched with food. But the restaurants and coffee shops that specialize in rolls and coffee determined that even dark roasts have enough acidity to make a good match.

Does the correlation between red and white wine and certain food exist between light and dark roast coffees and certain foods? Sweetness, complexity, and bitter notes called tannins most frequently influence a wine/food match. In this way, coffee is similar. But whereas red wines often contain more tannins and are *more* complex than white wines, dark roast coffees often contain more tannins but are *less* complex than light roasts. As with wine, coffee/food matching is an endless discussion with myriad possibilities.

Consider these two key questions when planning a menu that includes coffee:

Q: Will you serve the coffee during the meal or after with dessert?

A: When served with a meal, the coffee must complement the main course. For example, a light roast would pair nicely with a meat course such as steak. A darker roast would pair better with lighter fare. Dessert coffees can be lighter bodied (of either dark or light roast), with a weaker flavor, and may include liqueurs.

Coffee's a great after-dinner beverage. Some dieticians claim that cold beverages interfere with digestion—and that hot ones do not—making coffee a good choice to cap off a meal. If you don't serve dessert, a light-bodied coffee adds a delicate note and can enhance digestion.

Q: Will the coffee's flavor overpower the foods?

A: Don't choose coffee to complement your food and then brew it so that it overpowers, or on the other end of the spectrum, it gets lost amidst the food flavors. Heavier bodied coffee will stand up to foods more easily. Save lighter bodied, more delicate coffees for serving alone or with light foods.

Darker roasts, with their tannic flavors, pair well with higher-fat foods. Light roasts, apt to be complex, pair well with lighter foods because their complexity makes them seem like an added course. Foods containing salt and fat tend to neutralize the coffee's acidity, making harsh coffees a good match to a croissant with butter.

Serving Temperature

Wine experts often tell us that people drink wines at temperatures too cold or too warm to enjoy its full flavor. The same can be true of coffee. Coffee is likely around 180°F (82°C) or hotter when it reaches your cup. Experts often wait a few minutes before drinking, knowing that the mouth's ability to recognize the full flavor palate increases when a liquid is slightly cooler. Most experts agree that 140° F (60°C) is an ideal temperature to discern coffee's complexity. That said, it is always good form to serve coffee as soon as possible after brewing.

ADD CREAM TO YOUR COFFEE OR COFFEE TO YOUR CREAM?

This age old controversy actually has a scientific answer. Add cream to your cup and then pour in the coffee. Why? The combined mass of cream and coffee together loses energy to the surrounds, which lowers its temperature. The hotter the initial temperature, the faster the drink loses energy. The temperature starts lower when the cream enters the cup first, so the drink loses energy slower. This means the coffee will keep its heat longer.

Sugar and Milk: Coffee's Complements or Nemeses?

Sugar

Sugar's popularity in coffee stems from the syrupy viscosity it creates as it melts. No artificial sweeteners offer this change. Natural cane sugar tastes best. It has a low melting-point, absorbs fewer extraneous and undesirable odors, and blends easily. An oft-cited industry-circulated story about U.S. coffee drinkers suggests that sugar use rivals milk use in its popularity in the United States. But coffee connoisseurs remain divided about its use.

Some say that coffee itself is sweet enough and that sugar simply adulterates the drink. Others claim that coffee should be enjoyed sweetened and lightened to taste, stating that it's no different than putting a good sauce on fish. I say do what your taste buds desire. Don't drink your coffee to please anyone but you.

You do have other choices of sweetener besides sugar. In coffee terms, all sweeteners—including sugar—are artificial because coffee itself has some natural sugars. Here are a few of the most popular sweeteners:

Aspartame

After a study showed a possible link between sodium saccharin and cancer, aspartame came on the scene. It not only seemed completely safe, but it didn't have any bitter aftertaste, which some saccharin users reported. This made it ideal for coffee.

To this day, it is highly regarded as a sugar substitute, although some studies claim the body can convert it to ethanol, making it potentially dangerous in high amounts. (This controversy, as all others, is beyond the scope of this book.) Aspartame doesn't work well for baking because it loses heat—not of concern to the relatively short heat cycle of brewed coffee.

Sucralose

After controversial research predicted that aspartame, when ingested in large quantities, can turn into ethanol, sweetener users sought a more natural alternative. Sucralose, better known as Splenda, came out first. It has won vast marketplace acceptance for being "made from sugar," although it has not yet displaced aspartame. It has its own fans and detractors. Critics claim it is no longer natural in its final form.

Stevia

Stevia has seemingly everything going for it. It is natural, made from a leaf, and even has roots in ancient third-world cultures. However, minimal research has been done on it, and it currently has relatively small market penetration. To its fans, it seems perfect. Its detractors claim it hasn't been scrutinized enough. As a sweetener, some coffee drinkers claim it does not sweeten coffee as do sugar or other alternatives.

Sodium saccharin

Sodium saccharin has been around since the 1870s. It gained popularity during World War I when sugar was in short supply, but it really hit its stride during the 1960s when dieting became all the rage. After a death blow from a highly publicized study linking sodium saccharin to cancer in rats, it quickly lost its reputation, was superseded by aspartame, and is now cheap. Interestingly, though, no one seems to fear it any more. As a coffee sweetener, it is not popular because of its bitter, metallic aftertaste.

Coffee additions: Cream in a pitcher, sugar in a bowl, flavors in shot glasses. Are they ingredients or adulterants? Sugar has been added to coffee virtually since the discovery. Milk has been added since its introduction to Europe.

Milk

There's a theory that France had a better coffee reputation than England purely due to its more plentiful, richer milk. At least that was the case during the 1700s. Today, the world's largest coffee chains spend more money on milk than on coffee.

So which milk complements coffee the best? For brewed, filtered coffee, experts say cream with higher fat content, sometimes called 18 percent cream, light cream, or coffee cream taste best. Milk—even whole milk—has considerably less fat content, so you need more of it to deliver the same taste combination. Soy milk acts similarly to whole milk. Non-dairy coffee creamers, with their high sodium content, were designed to counteract the taste of harsh, cheaper Robusta coffee.

Espresso milk-based beverages, such as cappuccinos and lattes, taste best when made with rich, full-fat milk. In these drinks, choice of milk improves more than just flavor. Milk's fat actually causes it to stretch during frothing and allows it to reach the best consistency, a great virtue in cappuccinos and lattes.

NO SODIUM CITRATE

Find 18 percent cream without sodium citrate (examine the ingredients list). This ingredient neutralizes acid. You may have to contact a local dairy—and you won't believe the taste difference.

Flavored Coffee

Sugar, sweeteners, and milk aren't the only coffee additives. The flavored coffee age as we know it began in the 1960s when instant coffees producers began adding artificial flavors such as vanilla and hazelnut to their drinks. But actually, flavoring coffee goes back much further in history.

To stretch coffee quantities, some people blended coffee with a variety of grains. The major U.S. coffee port city of New Orleans, for example, popularized chicory-flavored coffee, made by adding to the drink a slightly bitter tree bark.

Roasting companies have successfully added hazelnut, vanilla, and chocolate to their coffees. In the 1980s, many a specialty coffee bean shops smelled predominantly like hazelnut, not coffee, which shows hazelnut's influence and popularity as a coffee flavor additive.

These flavorings can be natural or artificial. They typically get added after roasting by tossing the beans in a cylinder with syrups. The flavoring then coats the still-hot beans, which can sometimes appear glossy in the final product.

I recommend adding flavors at home. If you know you enjoy just one type of flavored coffee, consider coffees flavored by your roaster. Just know that your grinder and brewing equipment will likely take on the tastes and aromas of that flavor. Some grocery stores have two grinders, one for flavored and the other for unflavored, to address this issue.

Steaming and Frothing Milk

Perfectly frothed and steamed milk for espressos is as important as a perfect shot. Even the most die-hard purist can't resist the taste and viscosity of a perfectly made cappuccino. I purposefully separated this section from the espresso because it's a different art form. I also chose to focus on drinks that anyone with a good home espresso machine could make. Though a commercial machine may feature a more powerful steam wand, a home machine can produce frothed and steamed milk that's just as good. I fully expect to be wowed by the drinks you make after just a few practice runs.

Start with a nice cold pitcher for milk for steaming and frothing.

Latte Steaming and Frothing Tutorial

A latte requires steamed milk, but little or no foam. The goal is to time your steam wand's rise to the milk's surface so that the milk is hot, rich, and creamy all at the same time. With practice (using the steps below), you will achieve this every time.

Not everyone wants foam. To reduce or minimize foam, rap the milk pitcher on a tabletop or other hard surface every once in awhile as you keep the steam wand submerged.

Materials

These materials work for frothing and steaming milk for cappuccinos and lattes. We will not repeat them in the cappuccino or macchiato tutorials.

Chilled stainless steel pitcher

Milk, any kind, from non-fat to half and half, though whole milk offers the best results

Espresso machine set to "steaming/frothing" setting

Spoon, optional

Damp towel

1-ounce (30 ml) shot of espresso

ATTENTION SINGLE BOILER ESPRESSO MACHINE OWNERS

If you have a single boiler machine, you may want to froth and steam milk *before* making your espresso shots. This type of machine has a one-bto two-minute delay when switching from coffee making to milk frothing to let the boiler come up to temperature.

< A café latte is the most popular of all milk-based espresso drinks. The steamed milk is key, although the foam on top offers an important visual impact and texture.

A MISTAKE TO AVOID

This photo demonstrates a common mistake. Bobbing the pitcher up and down by steaming/frothing will result in oversized bubbles. This also happens when the wand comes fully out of the milk and steam shoots down from above. The goal is dense creamy foam, not loose bubbles.

Instructions

1. Fill the pitcher with milk no more than half way to leave room for expansion **(a)**.

2. Place the pitcher under the steam wand. Fully submerge wand's tip and bring it near to pitcher's bottom.

3. Turn steam on full power.

4. Lower the pitcher slowly. Stop when the wand's tip sits just under the milk's surface **(b)**. When steam is on, never remove the wand completely from the milk.

5. If you desire foam, hold the wand tip just under the milk's surface. Keep your hand on the pitcher. If the milk takes a long time to heat up, push the wand's tip back down near the pitcher's bottom. This will allow you to finish heating the milk without excessive frothing. Once the pitcher is almost too hot to hold, you are finished steaming.

6. After each steaming, immediately wipe the wand with a damp cloth **(c)**. With the cloth wrapped around wand, shoot a few steam jets to thoroughly expel any milk residue **(d)**. Be careful not to burn your hand.

Latte Steaming and Frothing Tutorial

a

b

c

d

Cappuccino Steaming and Frothing Tutorial

A cappuccino is technically one-third frothed milk, one-third steamed milk, and one-third espresso. But this equation is almost never a reality. Don't focus on the ratios. Instead, concentrate on getting the milk steamed and creating enough foam to define a cappuccino before the steam pitcher gets too hot. You'll make some great drinks. With time and practice, you'll fine tune your own signature ratio.

The materials for this are the same as the materials under the latte tutorial.

Instructions

The instructions for steaming and frothing milk for cappuccino are identical to those for the latte. The ratio of espresso to milk and cappuccino's use of frothed milk are the main differences.

To froth and steam milk for a cappuccino, follow the latte instructions through step 5 and then jump in here.

1. Free pour the steamed milk into the espresso using a spoon to hold back the foam (a, b, c).

2. Using the same spoon, top with foam (d, e).

Café Macchiato Steaming and Frothing Tutorial

The macchiato is perhaps the easiest to make of all milk-based espresso drinks. It is simply an espresso shot to which you add some frothed milk. Put another way, it's a super dry cappuccino with very little foam. In Italy, they say it is stained with milk. It contains no steamed milk.

Instructions

To froth milk for a café macchiato, follow the above latte instructions through step 5, then jump in here. Note: You will not use the steamed milk but only a bit of foam.

1. Using a spoon, take out a small amount of foam, no more than a dollop.

2. Place it atop the espresso.

Cappuccino Tutorial

A good *dry* cappuccino contains almost no steamed milk, just foam. It is easy to see the difference when comparing this photo to the standard cappuccino.

Coffee Recipes: Brews, Cocktails, and Beyond

There are so many coffee drinks out there that you could create an entire book of them. For this chapter, I've chosen a few of my favorites.

Espresso. Note the brown crema on top: at casual glance it might appear to be cream, but It's coffee, pure coffee!

🫘 Espresso

As French diplomat Charles-Maurice de Talleyrand-Périgord once said, "Espresso should be as black as the Devil, as hot as hell, as pure as an angel, and as sweet as love." See chapter 6, which begins on page 127, for more about Espresso.

1 ounce (30 ml) of espresso
Sugar, to taste

1. Prewarm the espresso cup, saucer, and spoon.
2. Place the espresso cup under the coffee spout.
3. Prepare an espresso.
4. Serve with sugar, to taste, if desired.

Serving suggestion: Serve with a glass of still water.

Serving size: 1 espresso shot

🫘 Cappuccino

A cappuccino is technically one-third espresso, one-third warm milk, and one-third milk foam, but the ratio often changes to meet the espresso maker's tastes. The word cappuccino likely derives from the Capuchin monks. The cap of milk foam resembles a monk's hood (*capuccio*). The color of the monks' hoods also recalls the beverage's brown hue.

1 ounce (30 ml) espresso
1 cup (240 ml) milk
Spoon

1. Prepare an espresso shot and place it into a cup.
2. Steam and froth the milk.
3. Free pour the milk onto the espresso shot.
4. Using a spoon, add foam to the top. Milk foam will separate to create the perfect cap.

Serving suggestion: Decorate the cappuccino by drizzling chocolate sauce on top, using a wooden skewer to make designs.

Serving size: 1 cappuccino

🫘 Dry Cappuccino

A dry cappuccino is composed of espresso with layered milk foam. The amount of steamed milk, however, is significantly less than in a regular cappuccino.

1 ounce (30 ml) espresso
Milk foam, to taste

1. Prepare an espresso shot and place it into cup.
2. Steam the milk.
3. Using a spoon, add foam to the top of the espresso.

Serving suggestion: Enjoy with any sort of sweet treat or dessert.

Serving size: 1 dry cappuccino

Cappuccino. Note the white cap and the layers of espresso beneath, clearly visible though a glass mug.

Café Latte

Often served for breakfast, this white coffee consists of coffee and hot milk served with a little milk foam. The Swiss affectionately call it *schale*, which literally translates to "bowl."

1 ounce (30 ml) espresso

1 cup (240 ml) milk

1. Prepare an espresso shot and place it into a cup.
2. Steam and froth the milk.
3. Free pour milk into espresso shot.
4. Put foam on top of milk. Foam should be thick and will separate to create the perfect latte.

Serving suggestion: On a hot day, make the iced version of this drink by allowing your 1-ounce (30 ml) espresso shot to cool before pouring it over a glass filled with ice. Add 1 cup (240 ml) of cold milk and stir.

Serving size: 1 café latte

Café Mocha

Like a latte, the café mocha is one-third espresso, two-thirds milk, but with cocoa powder or chocolate syrup. Don't be fooled by the word "mocha" however. It originally described a town in Yemen—and had nothing to do with chocolate. Today it has taken on new meaning, popularized to describe a drink that contains chocolate.

1 ounce (30 ml) espresso

1 tablespoon (6 g) sweet cocoa powder or 1 tablespoon (20 g) chocolate syrup

1 cup (240 ml) milk

1. Prepare an espresso shot.
2. Place the cocoa powder or chocolate syrup in cup.
3. Pour in the espresso and stir.
4. Steam the milk and add to the drink.

Serving suggestion: For a chocolaty refreshment, make up the iced version of this drink. Make a 1-ounce (30 ml) espresso and allow it to cool. Pour 1 tablespoon (5 g) cocoa powder or 1 tablespoon (20 g) chocolate syrup into a glass and then mix with espresso, ice, and 1 cup (240 ml) cold milk.

Serving size: 1 café mocha

Café Latte

Café Mocha

Iced Café Latte

Iced Café Mocha

Americano

This drink, made by combining espresso with boiling water, is sometimes called a café americano. Switch out cold water for hot water to create the iced version.

1 ounce (30 ml) espresso
5 ounces (140 ml) boiling water

1. Prepare an espresso shot and pour into a cup.
2. Add boiling water and stir.

Serving suggestion: Pour the hot water in first and then top with espresso rather than the other way around. It takes slightly more effort, but it preserves the crema.

Serving size: 1 café americano

Red Eye

Ever wonder what would happen if you combined regular drip coffee with espresso? The result is the red eye, named for its ability to keep you up at night and called various names depending on the region, including "Shot in the Dark" in the Pacific northwest.

5 ounces (150 ml) hot black coffee, any brew
1 ounce (30 ml) espresso

1. Make 1 cup of freshly brewed drip coffee.
2. Make 1 espresso shot.
3. Combine them together and stir.

Serving suggestion: Make a Black Eye by adding a second, 1-ounce (30-ml) espresso shot. Add a third 1-ounce (30 ml) shot to get a Dead Eye.

Serving size: 1 red eye

Macchiato

Don't confuse this with the drink made by some specialty coffee chains. Macchiato, also called spotted espresso, is an espresso crowned with a small dome of foamed milk.

1 ounce (30 ml) espresso
1 tablespoon milk foam

1. Prepare an espresso shot.
2. Prepare the milk foam in a separate receptacle.
3. Add 1 tablespoon of milk foam to the top of the espresso.

Serving suggestion: The small espresso cups cool very rapidly. Prewarm the espresso cup, saucer, and spoon to preserve the drink's heat. Also, don't stir. The visual of this drink is part of its allure.

Serving size: 1 macchiato

Caramel Macchiato

As its name suggests, this drink is a version of the macchiato with added caramel, popularized by a specialty U.S. coffee chain.

1 ounce (30 ml) espresso
1 cup (240 ml) milk, steamed
Vanilla syrup, to taste
Caramel sauce, to taste

1. Prepare an espresso shot and steam the milk.
2. Place vanilla syrup in a cup.
3. Free pour steamed milk over the syrup.
4. Using a spoon, top the steamed milk with foam.
5. Pour freshly brewed espresso through foam into cup.
6. Drizzle the top with caramel sauce.

Serving suggestion: In the mood for something cold? Try an iced caramel macchiato. Prepare two 1-ounce (30 ml) espresso shots and let them cool. In a pint or iced tea glass, squeeze in vanilla syrup to taste. Fill the glass three-fifths of the way with milk (approximately 1 cup [240 ml]). Add ice almost to the top. Pour the espresso shots over ice and top with whipped cream and caramel.

Serving size: 1 caramel macchiato

Americano

Macchiato

Red Eye

Caramel Macchiato

☕ Espresso con Panna

This drink, a single or double shot of espresso, literally translates from Italian to mean "espresso with cream." The simple addition of whipped cream creates a whole new espresso drink.

One or two 1-ounce (30 ml) espresso shots

Whipped cream, to taste

1. Prepare an espresso shot.
2. Pour into a cup.
3. Top with whipped cream, to taste.

Serving suggestion: This drink is perfect served with any flavor ice cream, though vanilla accentuates the coffee's flavor. Unlike flavored coffee, vanilla ice cream complements rather than competes for the coffee's aroma.

Serving size: 1 espresso con panna

☕ Espresso Martini

This coffee drink is a take on the classic martini cocktail. It's best when shaken, not stirred.

1 ounce (30 ml) espresso, cold

1½ ounces (45 ml) vodka

1½ ounces (45 ml) coffee liqueur

1 ounce (30 ml) white crème de cacao

1. Prepare an espresso and let it cool.
2. Once cool, combine with other ingredients in a martini shaker filled with ice.
3. Shake it (don't stir it).
4. Strain into a chilled martini glass. The drink should appear somewhat frothy.

Serving suggestion: For a nice touch, add cocoa power to the rim of your martini glass before serving.

Serving size: 1 espresso martini

☕ Irish Coffee

This drink works best if you have a drip brew machine and an espresso maker so you can froth the whiskey before adding it to the coffee. Whiskey gives the drink its implied provenance.

2 teaspoons (8 g) raw sugar

1 ounce (30 ml) Irish whiskey (alcoholic)

1/2 cup (120 ml) freshly brewed coffee, any brew

2 tablespoons (30 g) semi-whipped cream

1. Attach the steam wand to your espresso maker.
2. Add the sugar and whiskey to a glass.
3. Place frothing nozzle into the whiskey and make steam for about 5 seconds to heat.
4. Prepare fresh coffee. Combine it with the warm whiskey.
5. Top the coffee with whipped but slightly runny cream.

Serving suggestion: Don't mix an Irish coffee. It is intentionally served without a spoon so that the sugar, coffee, and whiskey mix only by tilting the glass. To enjoy Irish coffee the old-fashioned way, sip it through the cold cream.

Serving size: 1 Irish coffee

Espresso con Panna

Irish Coffee

Espresso Martini

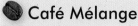 Café Mélange

By Daniel Heiniger

Unlike the espresso con panna, which adds whipped cream to espresso, the café mélange is a meltingly creamy combination of brewed drip coffee and this whipped treat.

1/2 cup (120 ml) freshly brewed coffee, any brew

1 tablespoon (4 g) whipped cream

1 teaspoon (3 g) grated chocolate or 1 teaspoon (2 g) cocoa powder

1. Prepare brewed coffee.

2. Top with whipped cream.

3. Dust with grated chocolate or cocoa powder.

Serving suggestion: Make a mint café mélange by adding mint extract or a mint leaf. Garnish with mint leaves for added visual appeal.

Serving size: 1 café melange

Recipe copyright Jura, www.jura.com

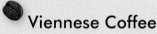 Pepresso

By Daniel Heiniger

Beware: This fiery espresso has kick. As chocolate flavored with pepper found its way into the mainstream, so too has pepresso, a sweet yet spicy blend of chocolate, pepper, and espresso sure to bewitch the senses.

1 ounce (30 g) chocolate sauce

Mixed peppercorns in a peppermill, ground, to taste

1 ounce (30 ml) espresso

1. Coat an empty espresso cup with chocolate until the base of the cup is well covered.

2. Season the chocolate with a little freshly ground pepper.

3. Place the espresso cup under the coffee spout.

4. Prepare the espresso shot in the chocolate-pepper cup.

Serving suggestion: Before serving your pepresso, stir it well to maximize the pepper-chocolate-espresso flavor.

Serving size: 1 pepresso

Recipe copyright Jura, www.jura.com

Café Royale

This recipe appears in a Perry Mason film *The Velvet Claws*, starring the great Warren William. The film is bizarre, but the drink is fascinating.

1/2 cup (120 ml) freshly brewed coffee, any brew

1 teaspoon (4 g) granulated cane sugar

2 ounces (60 ml) brandy

2 ounces (60 ml) heavy cream

1. Pour hot, freshly brewed coffee into a cup or glass.

2. Add the granulated sugar. Stir until it dissolves.

3. Add the brandy and stir again.

4. Over the back of a teaspoon, pour heavy cream over the top of the drink so that it floats. Serve immediately.

Serving suggestion: For a non-alcoholic version of this coffee, substitute fruit juice or light-flavored coffee syrup such as apricot for the brandy.

Serving size: 1 café royale

Viennese Coffee

By Daniel Heiniger

This sweet temptation with its vanilla ice cream and syrup probably won the heart of Empress Elisabeth of Vienna.

½ cup (120 ml) freshly brewed coffee, any brew

Vanilla flavored syrup, to taste, optional

1 scoop vanilla ice cream

1. Brew the coffee but not too far ahead of making the drink that the pot will finish brewing.

2. Add vanilla flavored syrup, if desired, to a tapered glass.

3. Shape a round scoop of vanilla ice cream and add to the glass.

4. Place the glass under the coffee spout.

5. Let the coffee flow directly down the edge into the glass, over the ice cream. Serve immediately.

Serving suggestion: Garnish with grated chocolate and serve with a short straw.

Serving size: 1 Viennese coffee

Recipe copyright Jura, www.jura.com

🫘 Iced Coffee

You likely have some brewed coffee left over from breakfast. Why not pour it over ice for an afternoon treat? You can either let it sit out for a few hours or take it off the warming plate, pour it into a pitcher, and put it into the fridge. It's good for the environment too because it extends the product's life.

6 ounces (140 ml) freshly brewed dark roast coffee

Ice

1 teaspoon sweetener, to taste, optional

Milk, to taste, optional

1. Brew a pot of dark-roasted coffee.

2. Let the coffee stand at room temperature for 3 to 5 hours or refrigerate until cold, about 1½ to 3 hours.

3. Fill a tall glass with ice cubes.

4. Pour the chilled coffee into the glass, over ice.

5. Stir the coffee to equalize its temperature.

6. Add milk and sweetener, if desired.

Serving suggestion: Freeze some of your morning's coffee in ice cube trays. That way, the cubes won't dilute the coffee. Also, try cold cream in your iced coffee. It will taste a little bit like a milk shake. Take it one step further and enjoy a scoop of ice cream with this drink—not in it but on the side.

Serving size: 1 iced coffee

Iced Coffee

Mexican Coffee

The name for this drink comes from the Mexican tradition of spicing up food and drink (often in an attempt to preserve food *and* make it taste delicious). The use of white tequila gives this drink some flare.

1 ounce (30 ml) coffee liqueur

1 ounce (30 ml) white tequila

5 ounces (150 ml) freshly brewed hot black coffee, any brew

1 teaspoon (5 g) brown sugar, or to taste

1½ ounces (15 g) whipped cream

Grated chocolate, to taste

1. Combine the liqueur, tequila, and coffee in a large coffee cup.
2. Sweeten to taste with brown sugar.
3. Gently float the whipped cream on top.
4. Sprinkle with grated chocolate.

Serving suggestion: Add 1/2 teaspoon (1 g) ground cinnamon or a cinnamon stick for another traditional variation on this drink.

Serving size: 1 Mexican coffee

Café au Lait

Café au lait is French for "coffee on milk." It's a traditional morning drink in France. It became popular elsewhere when tourists visited the country and brought back the drink. It's one of the original fun drinks.

½ cup (120 ml) French Roast coffee

½ cup (120 ml) milk

1. Brew French Roast coffee.
2. Steam the milk.
3. Pour equal parts coffee and steamed milk into a cup.
4. Mix and serve hot.

Serving suggestion: For a traditional New Orleans–style drink, brew the coffee with 1 tablespoon of chicory.

Serving size: 1 café au lait

Odd but Interesting Brewing Methods

Now that I've instructed you on the most popular methods, here are a few preparation methods difficult to find anywhere else. Francis Thurber, in his 1880 book *Coffee: From Plantation to Cup,* records a few notable brewing recipes. Today, they are more than a hundred years old. Here, they are reprinted for your pleasure. If you were a wealthy world traveler in Thurber's time, this is what you would likely drink. (Note, the coffee recipes below appear as Thurber printed them, meaning they may not be as complete as the recipes we provided earlier in this chapter.)

French Coffee: Café Noir

French coffee pot (author's note: presumably a manual drip pot)
2 tablespoons (10 g) coffee
Boiling water
Milk, optional

1. Grind coffee.
2. Pack grounds solidly in the coffee pot (the regular French filtering pattern).
3. Pour boiling water, passing it two or three times through the coffee pot.
4. For café au lait, add hot milk in a 3-to-1 ratio of milk to coffee.

Serving suggestion: For flavor, add ½ tablespoon of powdered chicory to grinds before brewing. Thurber claims that many French families saved their morning coffee's spent grounds, ran more hot water through them, and saved the water for coffee later that day.

Brazil/Rio Coffeehouse Prep

In the 1870s, Brazilians roasted most of their coffee in open pans and made it using a larger, but non-specific, grounds-to-water ratio. Thurber claims that the local Brazilian epicureans sought coffee kept "five or six years in the hull." He writes, "It is claimed by good judges that there is no coffee in the world superior to old Rio preserved in the hull until mellowed by age. It develops a richness, and at the same time a delicacy of flavor not found in any other variety of the bean."

Old Government Java Recipe (aka Café Au Lait à la Hollandaise)

Thurber did not write this recipe but obtained it from an old resident in Batavia, a Javan city. It records the then-outdated coffee preparation method favored by Dutch settlers in Java.

1. Take coffee pot composed of two detached parts, a metal drip maker with an upper filter using fine holes (like a salt shaker).
2. Place a flannel cloth filter over the upper section's bottom, covering it completely.
3. Add a sufficient quantity of well-ground coffee and firmly tamp.
4. Slowly pour cold water onto the grounds and allow it to drip completely through the filter, into the reservoir below. This will likely take 4 or 5 hours. Keep the filter high, narrow, and fully packed to retard the flow.
5. Mix the finished extract with hot milk in a 1-to-3 ratio of coffee extract to hot milk.

< Mexican Coffee

Resources

Years ago, most books on coffee would feature a list coffee roasters, manufacturers, and appliance retailers for buying supplies. That has all changed with the growth of the online marketplace and the sheer number of craft roasters. To be fair to the various suppliers, I have kept this list short and, with a few exceptions, limited it to noncommercial websites and organizations.

Online Resources

There are now so many consumer review sites that it is a challenge to find credible, objective information on products. Many reviews are written by nontechnical consumers who are awed by the new-car smell of a new product or soured by buyers' remorse. Beware of putting too much credence in a review until you discern a reviewer's credentials and testing methodology. Here are a few top coffee sites that pass inspection.

www.coffeegeek.com
An early forum that has grown into a significant worldwide community of end-users. Anyone can post reviews, so they vary in reliability and usefulness. A lot of the forum is devoted to a close-knit band of hobbyists in the community.

www.coffeereview.com
Founded by author Kenneth Davids, the Coffee Review focuses chiefly on reviewing coffee bean varietals by a wine-testing scale. Davids is honest, but, if anything, he's prone to grading everyone a "C" or above. As in wine taste tests, they are subjective, and you must learn to calibrate reviewers' tastes with your own.

http://home.planet.nl/~rjeroenv/index.htm
This great website features Mr. Robert Vriesendorp's reviews and commentary, as well a small-but-fun treasure chest of photos of coffee gear. Joerens has useful testing methodology.

www.coffeecompanion.com
This is my website, and it features in-depth technical reviews of brewers, grinders, and other gear, plus occasional feature articles about coffee or commentaries on coffee issues.

Equipment and Supplies

Here are just a few commercial recommendations, since they offer gear that is difficult to obtain and gear you're not likely to find in local brick-and-mortar stores.

www.sweetmarias.com
This online retailer focuses primarily on unroasted (green) coffee beans and home roasters, some brewers, and a whole lot of information. Naturally enough, they tend to recommend what they sell, but they seem to sell almost everything. Their tutorials are very detailed, and may overwhelm the newbie home coffee roasters.

www.greencoffeebuyingclub.com
This informal group doubles as a buyers' club where small end-users pool their resources to group buy some top quality green beans. Prices are competitive, and they have a good reputation.

Magazines

Tea and Coffee Trade Journal
Monthly magazine for the trade, but with many articles of aficionado interest and international perspective.

Books

I have not read every book there is about coffee, only most of them. The following are some personal favorites.

Coffee: A Guide to Buying, Brewing, and Enjoying, Fifth Edition (Paperback) by Kenneth Davids
ISBN-13: 978-0-31224-665-5
Kenneth Davids has written several books, but this is the first. Each edition has been substantially updated so if you have the time or resources, consider checking

out each one. Ken is an affable hippie who ran his own coffee store in the 1960s and 1970s. He like brewers but he loves varietals. He runs a website currently, where he reviews coffee beans (see above). Any book by Davids is highly recommended.

Coffee Floats and Tea Sinks by Ian Bersten
ISBN-13: 978-0-64609-180-8
If you ever see this at a library sale, grab it. At last check, it sells for a small fortune on Amazon or eBay. It's a glorious coffee (and tea) book, filled with opinions, but mostly wise ones. Bersten, who is Australian, has a great writing style and a global focus.

Coffee and Tea by Peter Quimme
This 1970s book is perhaps out of date, but it has a lot of good information, and until I found Ken Davids books, I found it the most useful of the many books. It is a tiny pocket-sized book, and I used to carry it with me to coffee stores, as a guide to the beans and roasts.

Coffee by Joel Schipira
The Schipiras are a coffee-roasting family in upstate New York. They write a very nice testimonial to a business they obviously love, and some of the information is very useful. (They write from the perspective of pre-espresso and pre-specialty coffee culture.) As with Coffee and Tea, the varietal descriptions are limited—this was written before the current transportation methods and direct trade practices.

The Perfect Cup by Timothy Castle
Tim Castle is a member of the coffee trade, more specifically, he is an importer. His book is well written and useful, especially in capturing the essence of various coffee varietals, Castle's specialty.

The Complete Book of Coffee by Harry Rolnick
Rolnick was a trade writer who created a nice four-color book about coffee with great photos and graphics.

It is written with a special nod to Melitta, who was obviously very involved with its creation, and it portrays the world of coffee, pre-specialty, very well.

Joy of Coffee by Corby Kumner
ISBN-13: 978-0-61830-240-6

Kumner is a senior editor at the *Atlantic* magazine, and his articles for the *Atlantic* about coffee are world-class and enjoyable reads.

Espresso Coffee: Professional Techniques by David Schomer
Schomer founded Café Vivace, in Seattle. He is reputed to be an obsessive taskmaster and all-around perfectionist. In other words, my kind of guy. This book is recommended to anyone who wants to open an espresso shop for its practical information, though it is a great guide for espresso craftspeople and latte artists.

So, You Want to Go Into the Coffee Business…

Specialty Coffee Association of America
www.SCAA.org
If you are in the U.S., the Specialty Coffee Association of America (SCAA) is the leading small business organization dedicated to the trade. They hold a yearly conference that provides a clearing house of information, through its trade show and various seminars.

Specialty Coffee Association of Europe
www.scae.com
European-based specialty coffee association.

Norwegian Coffee Association
www.kaffe.no/?l=31&ls=32&h=301
They call themselves "Europe's coffee police." They set standards, certify gear, and even claim they make grocery store checks to monitor coffee quality.

Index

Acknowledgments

The following people have been so helpful and selfless in giving me their time, knowledge, and talents to create this book.

Ken Stevenson—Who sent a passionate enthusiast a plane ticket and introduced me to an industry.

Oren Bloostein of Oren's Daily Roast—My friend for many years, I still can't travel to Manhattan without visiting him and his Chemex.

Charlie Sarin of Coffee Express—For his insights and shared enthusiasm for collectibles.

Jim Reynolds of Peet's Coffee and Tea—Either doesn't know how to say no, or can't.

Erna Knutsen and John Rapinchuk—For inventing the term *specialty coffee*.

Donald Schoenholt of Gillies Coffee—Phone friend and coffee historian.

Christy Thorns of Allegro Coffee—The best coffee taste detective I've met.

Bob Heniken—Who made me the first cup of coffee that tasted as good as it smelled.

Ian Bersten, author, *Coffee Floats and Tea Sinks*—Historian par excellence

Liz Grassy of Chemex—For keeping the brewer alive.

Ken Davids, author, *Coffee*—For proving coffee is a viable topic for books.

Geoff Watts of Intelligentsia Coffee—For advancing the cause of selling in-season coffees and sharing his extensive photo library.

Mark Johnson of Intelligentsia Coffee—For his kind assistance during our photography shoot.

Frank Chambers—For his insights into coffee as an oil product, for testing my theories, and for giving me the ammo to take them public.

Scott Marquardt of Open Sky Coffee—For his passion for home roasting.

Dan Ephraim of Modern Process—For being the reigning expert on grinding.

Rasmy Buparat, Modern Process Lab Manager—For their countless grind tests.

Gery Smitt of Technivorm—For making the Volvo of brewers.

Aimee Markelz, Greg Fisher, Randy Pope, Bunn-O-Matic—For being a model company, and for your no-strings-attached help.

Joe Behm of Behmor Roasting—An inventor and kindred spirit.

George Howell of GH Coffee Company—Coffee visionary, fellow ENTP.

David Schomer of Café Vivace—For making espresso an engineering art.

Jim Cunningham of Cunningham Productions—For turning me onto espresso.

Carmen Cribari of Rancilio—For loaning the Rocky and Silvia, Chicago-style.

Angelo Forzano—For the loan of the wonderful La Pavoni piston espresso machine.

Linda Field of Capresso—If I ever can afford a PR person, you're it.

Randy Layton, Mike Johnson and David Boyd, of Boyds Coffee—For superior coffee packaging (which almost obviated the grinding chapter).

Joe Bean—For a little bit of everything.

Patricia Sinnott—For tasting all my experiments and for allowing me to take over the house with coffee gear (and personalities) over the years.

Edmund Preston Sinnott—For his espresso chapter expertise and demonstrations.

Shaun and Cameron Sinnott—For their continued indulgence in their father's eccentricity.

Marvin Hobbs—For keeping me sane.

Dr. Roberto Lang and Ann Ryan—For keeping me alive.

Rochelle Bourgault—For your saintly patience with me during the writing of this book.

Regina Grenier, Tom Petroff, Mary Studebaker and Michele Wilson—For your many hours working on the art and fact checking.

Margaret Swallow—For valuable insights regarding coffee botany that helped immeasurably.

About the Author

Kevin Sinnott, host of the how-to video *Coffee Brewing Secrets* and curator of the coffeecompanion.com website, is the U.S.'s foremost consumer coffee authority. His groundsbreaking Coffee Companion newsletter, which achieved a readership more than 10,000 strong, was the first publication to teach readers how to brew great tasting coffee, from water filters to coffee bean grinders to brewers. His latest project is missioncoffeecan, a web series following college students determined to win a national competition marketing their own brand of Guatemala coffee.